A LEARNING STAGE 3:
PROPERTY MANAGEMENT 101

By

Teresa Billingsley

ISBN-10: 1-946662-00-3
ISBN-13: 978-1-946662-00-2

Printed in the United States of America

Disclaimer

"A Learning Stage 3: Property Management 101" was written to provide accurate and current information for those who either are already in, or considering delving into the landlord - tenant arena. It is not intended to substitute for sound legal advice. If you have any legal questions, you should consult with a qualified attorney or expert to provide you with answers that apply to your particular situation.

The opinions expressed in this book are those of the author's and should not be construed as representing the opinions or policy of any official or agency. It is recommended that you read the relevant statutes and court decisions cited for clarification.

Dedication

I dedicate this book to my lord and savior, Jesus Christ, first and foremost. Second, in honor of the kindness my mother (Bertha Billingsley) has shown to everyone as a businesswoman, I pay homage to her as well. Finally, to the real estate community who strives to find ways to bridge the gap between consumers and professionals, I wrote this book for you.

Acknowledgement

I am grateful for the word of God. It provides wisdom and guidance in business and public relations. I strongly recommend The Bible as the primary source of sound counsel. If you are open and receptive to it, you will gain knowledge, understanding, humility and an uncanny ability to responsibly work with others and treat people respectfully.

My mother, my late grandparents, and other experienced landlords and managers taught me much about the rental industry. I choose to recognize you all with my deepest thanks.

Apartment associations employ and endorse advocates who represent real estate professionals' stance against unfair legislation. They facilitate workshops, training classes, legal updates, tips, trade magazines and notifications to landlords and managers for calls-to-action.

Law enforcement agencies who have carefully formed well put-together Crime Free Multi-Housing Programs (CFMHP) to educate the rental community are an asset to the neighborhoods they serve.

I would like to identify and salute all the above resources and acknowledge their incredible contributions. I recommend anyone interested in making their business the best it could possibly be to research the scriptures, learn from skilled veterans, and join and support your local apartment association and CFMHP.

Introduction

Please, recognize all anyone can do is to give you helpful information to empower you on your business journey. It is up to you to follow through and use the tools and resources given and presented to you to your advantage.

The material in this book is designed to help simplify the growth process for you. It is intended to entertain you while making controversial topics easier to navigate. It is meant to influence you to network and share with others who will also benefit.

I encourage you to also verify your understanding and interpretations of what you read, with the written laws in your state and jurisdiction. Attend tradeshows and classes where industry experts avail themselves to public inquiries.

Table of Contents

Disclaimer iv

Dedication vi

Acknowledgement viii

Introduction xi

Table of Contents xiii

10 Ways to Avoid Being the Test Case for a Discrimination Lawsuit..............1

15 Ways Applicants Dupe Landlords & Managers 7

4 Step Plan to Hire and Work with a Good Fit Management Company 12

5 Things Landlords Want from Vendors Working on Their Rental Properties 19

Role-Playing Scenarios
A Learning Stage 67 – Occupancy Standards 27

A Learning Stage 68 – Good Employee 30

A Learning Stage 69 – Give & Take Judgments 35

A Learning Stage 70 – 3 Landlords Lose 3-Day Notice Cases.....................41

A Learning Stage 71 – Fair Housing Rules 47

A Learning Stage 72 – Maddie 53

A Learning Stage 73 – Maintain a Balance 59

A Learning Stage 74 – Special Accommodation 63

A Learning Stage 75 – The Answer to Church 67

A Learning Stage 76 – Child's Play 71

A Learning Stage 77 – The Fill In 76

A Learning Stage 78 – Couples of Options 81

A Learning Stage 79 – Nightmare Pets 85

A Learning Stage 80 – Passing the Buck 91

A Learning Stage 81 – Comparable Difference 97

A Learning Stage 82 – Accentuate the Positive... 101

A Learning Stage 83 – Cletus Returns 107

A Learning Stage 84 – Judge Leslie 111

A Learning Stage 85 – Hands On Disaster 116

A Learning Stage 86 – Don't Alter My Security... 122

A Learning Stage 87 – Crime Free Help 129

A Learning Stage 88 – Plan to Change 135

A Learning Stage 89 – Discriminate Offenses 139

A Learning Stage 90 – Disability Dilemma.. 144

A Learning Stage 91 – Court Recovery? 149

A Learning Stage 92 – Pet Dilemma.. 154

A Learning Stage 93 – Surcharge.. 158

A Learning Stage 94 – Choosing Smart 161

A Learning Stage 95 – Critic Cal... 165

A Learning Stage 96 – Okay, Jose, Not!.. 172

A Learning Stage 97 – A New Perspective in Black and White.................... 177

A Learning Stage 98 – Language Barriers.. 182

A Learning Stage 99 – Advice of Contradiction 188

A Learning Stage 100 – Final Exam 194

A Learning Stage 101 – The Test of Time 201

Expert Query Log 205

10 Property Management Repair Alerts.. 211

4 Tangible Clues That Reveal Impropriety in Business 217

16 Signs of a Bitter vs. Better Employee 220

More Helpful Scriptures.. 225

Letter from the Author 238

PRAYER OF SALVATION 241

10 Ways to Avoid Being the Test Case for a Discrimination Lawsuit

Today, it is customary to place an online ad for free. As a result, ads are more loosely written with more verbiage. Landlords are no longer as strategic and concise, and post whatever they believe will attract the particular renters they seek.

Below is an example of a fairly typical ad a renter may read on the internet. Try the exercise below and test your skills on placing a good ad that would not spark a Fair Housing "*tester*" or "*secret shopper.*"

QUICK QUIZ

Question:

Can you spot some potential problems in the wording of the below ad?

Sample Ad:

1-bedroom apartment. Ideal for an older, retired couple. In a quiet building. No pets, no exceptions. Prefer married couple but two single adults OK. No children.

1

Private community with a sense of family. Across the street from St. Augustine's parish. A 5-minute walk to the best school in the neighborhood. Professionals only.

Answers:

These have all been identified by at least one Fair Housing organization as being discriminatory as they indicate a preference or limitation:

- Ideal for an older retired couple
- Quiet building
- No pets, no exceptions
- Prefer married couple
- Two single adults OK
- No children
- Private community
- With a sense of family
- St. Augustine's parish
- 5-minute walk
- Best school
- Professionals only

How well did you do? Now for what may create some slight confusion – you will find contradictory information in writing and at workshops held by Fair Housing. As an example, below are just five documents available online for you to review for yourself.

Document 1:
"Advertisements under 804(c) of the Fair Housing Act - Jan. 9, 1995"
http://www.fairhousing.com/index.cfm?method=page.display&pagename=HUD_resources_hudguid2

Document 2:
"For Rent: No kids! How Internet Housing Advertisements Perpetuate Discrimination"
http://www.nationalfairhousing.org/LinkClick.aspx?filetick et=zgbukJP2rMM%3D&tabid=2510&mid=8347
Document 3:
"Discriminatory Housing Ads Proliferate Online"
http://voices.washingtonpost.com/local-address/2009/05/discriminatory_housing_ads_pro.html
Document 4:
(Miami Valley) "Fair Housing Advertising Manual"
http://www.mvfairhousing.com/realtors/files/Fair%20Hous ing%20Advertising%20Manual.PDF
Document 5:
"Guidance Regarding Advertisements Under §804(c) of the Fair Housing Act"
http://www.hud.gov/offices/fheo/disabilities/sect804achte nberg.pdf

There are exemptions to certain preferential advertising, but they are limited. To review these exceptions, refer to Document 4 on pages 31-34.

Are you asking yourself the following questions?
1. I've used those words in my ads. If they are indeed discriminatory, why have I never had any trouble or violations for this before?
   - Perhaps because according to the National Fair Housing Association (NFHA), more than 7,500 discriminatory ads were identified, but only over 1,000 complaints were filed
   - Possibly because no one complained about your ad
   - Maybe because you had other inclusive language in your ad, so Fair Housing chose to give you the benefit of the doubt

- It could be that due to the high volume of discriminatory ads placed, you have evaded an investigation, but in this litigious age, don't expect to keep up such luck
- Although you used discriminatory language, it was not pursued by Fair Housing without knowing whether certain exemptions may have applied making it okay
- Your ad was reviewed by a Fair Housing investigator who was of the opinion it was not in violation
- Or your ad got Fair Housing's attention and they *shopped* you, but you did not convey any preferential treatment with the *testers* and no further action was taken
2. Some of these terms are not violations and I disagree. I have found documentation on the internet that indicates some of these words are acceptable.
    - You are right; you will find conflicting documents on some of these terms
    - For instance, the use of "quiet home," "quiet neighborhood" and "peaceful home" may be a clue that you are hinting you want to exclude families with children (see Document 3)
    - As an example of this point, Document 5 (page 4) & Document 1 state "quiet streets" are "not facially discriminatory and do not violate the Act."
    - The Fair Housing Center refer to "quiet" & "quiet neighborhood" as acceptable phrases (see Document 4 page 30)
    - Review Document 2, however, and see how many times "quiet" is listed in the few examples of actual discriminatory ads based on familial status (pages 15-16)

- I also have pamphlets/flyers I have collected from Fair Housing organizations in my area that discourage this language and view it as discriminatory
- A Fair Housing representative has said she would not file a lawsuit on this alone, but it could cause a *tester* or *secret shopper* to show up and investigate (see Document 3)

So what might you do to be in compliance and avoid being the test case for a discrimination lawsuit to minimize your liability?

1. Research and collect documents from reputable sources (Fair Housing, HUD, DOJ) with specific examples of what they consider and will pursue as being discriminatory language in advertising
2. Avoid using any words reliable sources have identified, regardless of opposing documents and opinions
3. Attend Fair Housing training in your area and directly ask the instructors to clarify any words or phrases you are confused about
4. Consult with a qualified attorney
5. Review cases of actual lawsuits
6. Take note of what complaints enforcing agencies say they will accept and pursue
7. Stick to safe language about the property and make no references or suggestions as to who the property would be best-suited for
8. Keep yourself informed and updated on this issue
9. When reputable sources give conflicting advice, choose the one that is safe. There is usually a clear, neutral choice – choose that one to avoid problems
10. Remember, discriminatory ads are not based on your intent, but founded on the consumer's reasonable perception of whether there is a Fair Housing violation

Above are suggestions to stay in compliance, avoid unnecessary liability, and to not draw attention to yourself and invite an investigation or *secret shopper*. However, you may feel justified to argue your right to use "quiet." After all, Document 1, written by a reputable source, indicates it is acceptable. You may feel so strongly about it you are willing to fight it out in court and spend thousands of dollars in legal fees to defend yourself. I say – it is certainly your choice to do so, but for me, until there is an undisputed consensus, I'll just use safe and unanimously acceptable language to fill my vacancy.

My goal is to obtain a qualified tenant with the least amount of conflict and roadblocks. This industry is demanding enough. For me, it's not about being right or fighting to prove a point at my own financial expense. Attorneys have shared their cases with other landlords where landlord clients have fought and won. One particular case, Fair Housing appealed and the landlord won the appeal. However, it cost over $90,000 to be told by two courts that the landlord was not in violation.

Is it worth nearly $100,000 to be told you are right, pay thousands in penalties and attorney fees to be told you are wrong, or avoid unnecessarily placing yourself in that position in the first place? I choose the latter. What is your pleasure?

15 Ways Applicants Dupe Landlords & Managers

In general, you can deter scammers by following proper protocol. Your best defense is utilizing solid guidelines and practices. It also helps to know some of the common scams being used and be on alert. Below is a list of fifteen frequently used tricks many swindlers try that you need to beware of.

The applicant may:
1. Intentionally not sign and/or date the application
- Their signature and date are your authorization to run checks and verify their information. If you conduct a check without them, they could state you did so *without* their permission.
2. Have a friend or they, themselves, impersonate their alleged employer, landlord, or references
- Ask questions that verify the veracity of the person's identity. For example, you may want to ask an employer to confirm his business address with you. A real employer should know that without hesitation, a friend posing as one's boss may not.
3. Express a sense of urgency to move in immediately
- Don't allow their panic to provoke you into cutting corners. If they have a legitimate emergency, then they should be *more* cooperative in supplying

anything you request more expeditiously. Often those with something to hide want you to quickly let them in, ask you to forego credit checks, or give excuses why they can't provide documented proof needed to qualify them.

4. Provide incorrect, incomplete, unverifiable or false information

- Carefully go over the application and don't accept it if pertinent information is missing or inconsistent. Is their cell number the same as their employer's number and one of their references? Why did they leave the address blank for their job of six years? These may be clues that they are not being completely honest and are withholding or concealing information on purpose.

5. Search for landlords who have no Application Procedure or written Resident Criteria, then lure the landlords or managers to engage in discriminatory conversation

- If a landlord takes the bait, the applicants can claim the owner did not accept their tenancy because he had a bias against them. For example, if the landlord made a point of discussing how many children would be moving in, it's inappropriate dialogue. The number of *children* is not a factor, the number of *occupants* are. By broaching this subject and not utilizing a fair written procedure or criteria, the landlord has now given them cause to argue how many children they had was the reason they were denied.

6. Offer immediate cash sensing the landlord's desperation

- Tricksters recognize that flaunting money is often a major temptation for landlords to become distracted. And most of the time that first set of funds is the last bit of money the landlord will ever see from the person. It is also often times monies the applicants saved up from not paying rent to their current or prior landlord.

7. Threaten to file a complaint or sue you if you don't accept them

- Refuse to cower to any intimidation tactics. If they are threatening you now and have not moved in, chances are they will become more problematic if accepted as tenants.

8. Either have someone with an impressive credit history pose as the applicant and apply for them, or use that person's information to get accepted

- Once you've accepted the application and move-in fees, you may never see their decoy again. The imposter served their intended purpose. Now a group of people with horrible credit that don't qualify move in until you realize the situation and evict them.

9. Promise the world to get the key and start moving in

- Refrain from providing a key to anyone until *after* you have thoroughly screened them and their deposit check has *cleared*. If you do it any other way you may dread your decision, for once they have access and move in, it will be difficult to get them out.

10. Present you with their own prepared documents (application, credit report, letters of references, employment information, etc.) and allege they cannot afford a credit check

- Use a reputable screening agent who is thorough. It has become easy to make and purchase fraudulent documents. Verify everything and only rely on respectable sources. Be consistent and rely on your own application and forms that you trust.

11. Contact you to apply for your vacancy and intentionally don't follow through. They wait for a period of time, and then file a discrimination complaint against you

- Too many landlords and managers fail to keep good documentation and this is what scammers and professional tenants rely on. Without a written policy that you consistently follow with each applicant, good documentation, or a rejection letter sent out, you will be unprepared to refute and defend against an accusation of discrimination. Often times you will not even recall the interaction without good notes.
12. Provide you with an overage of one thousand dollars of the amount you request to hold the rental for them
- They later point out their (*intentional*) mistake to you and request reimbursement. You discover their check is not good only after they have already cashed yours and scammed you out of $1,000.00.
13. Claim they are out of the country and unable to view the property & want to rent it
- Without meeting the applicant in person, you have no way of verifying who you are truly dealing with. These types of transactions are highly discouraged.
14. Get you to fill in part of the application for them
- If you input information on their application, it makes it difficult to say *they* lied when *you* are the one who wrote the information in.
15. Prompt you or a staff member to translate English instructions into their language
- It's best to have them supply their own translators of their choosing. This way they cannot later misrepresent what you told them or claim the translation was biased because it was done by you or one of your agents.

Con artists will try anything to get you to avoid doing due diligence and to violate the laws. You have no defense for inappropriate behavior. Ignorance of the law or saying you were duped into it are not viable excuses. You are held to a higher standard as the business professional to find out what the statutes are and to follow them.

4 Step Plan to Hire and Work with a Good Fit Management Company

It can be difficult to select a company to manage your rental properties. Where do you begin? How do you choose one business over another? This can be a daunting task without some guidance. This four-step plan should give you some direction to simplify making choices that might otherwise appear overwhelming.

I. Before You Decide to Hire
1. Know what you want.
    a. A company to set up your properties for you to manage
        i. It's best if you have the experience needed in order to do this well
    b. Tenant placement only
        i. If you're not up-to-date on the Fair Housing laws or do not have the time to handle this proficiently, it is better to hire someone to do this who is
    c. Full management services
        i. This option is suited for those who do not want to deal with all the tasks associated with the job, lack the knowledge, ability or interest to take on all that is involved

      ii. Be as diligent in screening management as you are when selecting tenants

      iii. Once you select one that will meet your needs, let them do their job

II. Where You Can Find Good Prospects

1. NARPM (National Association of Residential Property Managers) website
   a. http://www.narpm.org/search/search-managers.htm
2. Word of Mouth
3. Apartment Associations
4. Informative literature (articles, books, pamphlets, handouts, etc.) with industry tips and updates written by experts
5. Educational/Networking settings where they gather – seminars, training classes, tradeshows
6. Angie's List
   a. http://www.angieslist.com/
   b. *This is the only one that may cost you a fee to access their database*
7. Internet Search
8. Advertisements sent to you or your rental property
9. If you find a good company, but they are unable to take you on as a client, ask them for a referral

When you locate a few businesses that have piqued your interest, verify their licenses and check for complaints online at:

10. Bureau of Real Estate – *formerly named The Department of Real Estate (DRE)*
   a. http://www.dre.ca.gov/
11. Better Business Bureau
   a. http://www.bbb.org/
12. Search the worldwide web for reviews and any

information you can find on the company
a. http://www.yelp.com/
b. http://www.thumbtack.com/

III. Hiring – Screening Process

I recommend you formulate a list of a minimum of 3 good prospects. If you stop at one or two, you could limit your ability to better assess them and you may miss things you may want that others are offering.

You may prefer not to spend a lot of time researching the many companies out there, but be unaware of how to broaden the search. These are some common areas to target and compare to help you create a short list of companies that fall within the conditions you seek.

1. How long is the management contract for?
   a. Some would rather not be held to a lengthy contract
2. Review the Property Management Agreement
   a. Are you okay with the terms?
   b. Do you understand what is written?
   c. How do you terminate the contract if necessary?
3. Do they exercise good customer service skills?
   a. Are they attentive and professional?
4. Do their offers meet your needs and fit your criteria? You want a good balance. Here are some offers that have come under fire and should be weighed carefully:
   a. They promise to fill vacancies quickly
      o Not good if Fair Housing laws are violated
      o Not good if filled with problem tenants
      o Not good if the tenants are good, but do not stay very long

b. They take longer than the average companies to acquire tenants
  o Good if the tenants they place are first-rate, long-term tenants
  o Good if they are doing all they can and not many worthy prospects are applying
  o Not good if they are not being aggressively proactive in renting
  o Good if they recognize this is an area they need to work on and in the long run, they become much more proficient at it
c. Utilizing in-house staff for maintenance
  o Good if they are ethically operating with openness and transparency
  o Good if their staff are heavily supervised and they guarantee each job
  o Not good if they make a career of repairs and do not get your approval
  o Good if they do good work, at reasonable rates, with your authorization
  o Not good if bills are lacking and documentation is poor and selectively sent
  o Not good if they want total control and discourage you from getting a second opinion or using other qualified vendors on jobs
  o Not good if they add profit, mark-up cost, receive undisclosed kickbacks or commissions
d. Would you like a large, established company?
  o Good if they have more experienced staff and resources
  o Not good if they acquire too many clients and are unable to keep up
  o Not good if they have a high turnover rate of staff and you are frequently passed over to different people who are not updated on the status of your rentals

- o Not good if they are still operating under outdated methods and refuse to change
- e. Do you prefer a small, newly emerging company?
  - o Good when personal service is provided from loyal employees
  - o Good if eager to learn, grow and abide by the statutes that regulate them
  - o Good if they are passionate about their trade and bring fresh energy to it
  - o Good if they are starting out correctly and do not have old habits that need to be broken
  - o Good if their mission is to come up with innovative strategies and ideas to be an exceptional organization that is far superior than their competition
- f. Late fee collection
  - o Not good if the growing controversy and arguments against it are not understood
  - o Not good if the total amount goes to management because it might be an incentive for late rent collection
  - o Good if the entire amount goes to the property owner
  - o Not good if the owner would rather not collect late fees but management insists
5. What are your deal breakers?
   a. What is important to you in a company?
   - o Their reputation and credibility in the industry
   - o Professional website with online services
   - o Live person who answers the phone during business hours
   - o Availability to address emergencies 24 hours a day, 7 days a week
   - o Certifications, awards or endorsements from community leaders

o Reasonable & competitive rates
o Ongoing training – strive to exceed the mandatory standards
o Prompt responses
o Allow you to perform all repairs yourself or use your own trusted vendors
o All original receipts or invoices provided to you each month
o Regular and reliable documentation of accounting processes
o They listen to and address your concerns or questions in a timely manner
o Office location
o Experience and knowledge
o Size of the organization

6. Will they supply you with a list of references?
   a. Contact them personally and inquire as to their honest experiences

IV. After You Hire
1. Monitor how your property is being managed. Your due diligence and responsibilities have not ended.
   a. Do they respond to you in a reasonable amount of time?
   b. Are they treating your clients (tenants) fairly and professionally?
   c. Do they address repairs, discrepancies or other issues in a timely manner?
   d. Do they own up to their mistakes and immediately correct them?
   e. Are they fulfilling their contractual obligations?
   f. Are they acting in your best interest?
   g. Are your finances being handled properly?
   h. Are they violating any ethics codes or laws?
   i. Have they rejected offers to communicate better with you and resolve concerns you bring to their attention?

Remember this is business. You want to employ an agency to act on your behalf that has the skill and expertise to fulfill the duties required. This means not only being conscientious in acquiring and screening them, but also requires your continued due diligence in examining how the corporation performs. It will serve you well in the end and give you peace of mind to secure a professional organization that fits your criteria and meets your needs.

* The company websites listed are presented for your convenience and do not constitute an endorsement.

5 Things Landlords Want from Vendors Working on Their Rental Properties

Doing repairs on rental properties and interacting with tenants adds a whole new component to maintenance. Vendors who recognize the intricate skill and experience required to get the job done are an asset to rental property owners. If you master these 5 areas and consistently perform them well, you will make yourself more marketable.

1. Documentation is critical and useful if the matter goes to court
   - Dates and times of when you received the call and performed the service
   - Who got in touch with you – the tenant, management, or the landlord?
   - How were you contacted, by phone, text, or email?
   - What was the initial complaint reported?
   - Give your best price – no hidden fees, be reasonable
   - Photographs are extremely helpful
   - Describe the action taken or attempted
   - If the repair was not done as promised, immediately notify the owner why
     o Was the tenant uncooperative or a hindrance?

- o Did the residents refuse to let you in?
- o Had they forgotten about the appointment?
- o Did they not return your phone calls to set up an appointment time?
  - List the dates and times you tried to reach them
  - Were you unable to reach them for the scheduled confirmation call?
  - Always keep the owner updated of any problems

2. Helpful Observations
   - Being an extension of the owner's eyes and ears makes you valuable
   - When you got there what were your observations?
     - o Were there violations or other matters that need to be brought to the landlord's attention?
       - Smoke/Carbon Monoxide detectors disconnected or missing
       - Evidence of an unauthorized occupant/border or pet
       - Safety issues – hoarding, removal of fire extinguisher, loose step, etc.
   - Is the repair cost a result of the tenant's actions?
     - o Was a toilet stopped up by a child's toy belonging to the tenants
     - o Is an entry door broken because of a fight the tenants had with each other
     - o Are corrections needed because the residents made improper modifications to the unit
     - o Is there a bug infestation due to unclean conditions, old/spoiled food left out, unkempt premises or piles of dirty dishes all throughout?

3. Professional Interaction with the Residents

- Discuss only the job you are sent there to perform
  o Don't get personal
  o Refrain from giving any advice outside your scope of hire
- Try to cause the least bit of disturbance as possible
- Come prepared with your own tools
  o Do not bother or ask to borrow the tenant's property
- Avoid confrontations, arguments, and volatile situations – do not engage
- Treat everyone fair and equal
  o No flirting
  o No preferential treatment for those you have a romantic interest in
- Follow the rules/policies of vendor conduct
  o No wandering into areas where work is not being performed
  o Clean up after yourself, do not leave a mess
- Handle the call in an expedient and proficient manner
- If residents try to get workers to do other work not reported to the landlord
  o Politely explain you are only authorized and paid to be there to address that particular issue
  o Suggest they follow the repair policy and go through the proper channels

4. Assess a diagnosis of what caused the problem and options for repair. Explain it is...
   - an inexpensive fix but it's temporary (*Bandaid* solution)
   - what it will take to remedy the situation without getting a brand new replacement of equipment
   - your recommendation on how to handle it to get the owner's desired result and resolution

5. Pay Attention to Detail & Follow Instructions
   - Prioritize the repair – how emergent is it?
   - Abide by and be familiar with changes in the law affecting your trade (RRP rule - *http://www.epa.gov/lead*)
   - Are there any special instructions?
     o The tenant has an indoor pet, be careful it does not get out
     o Tenant has an outdoor pet, be sure not to let it in
     o Tenant left dog locked up in the garage, do not enter
     o No smoking on the premises
     o Do not leave doors wide open unnecessarily
     o Tenant wants to be present
     o Be careful not to move/rearrange items inside (*The owner may not want to disclose that the tenant may be visually impaired*)
     o Follow the parking rules & posted signs

Situational:

At a Fair Housing Workshop, an investigator relayed a case where a tenant complained her landlord was biased and discriminatory toward her and refused to make needed repairs because of her familial status. Management was asked for their side of the story so they reviewed their documented reports of their maintenance crew that showed they responded quickly to the request. They noted upon arrival no adults were present and a young girl answered the door in a towel after just exiting the shower. The girl was directed to have an adult call to reschedule and the workers left. It was against their written policy to be alone with a child who was not dressed.

Twice maintenance made the effort to reschedule and the tenant cancelled the appointments and did not initiate another visit.

Management sent a letter to the tenant articulating the attempts made to investigate and resolve the repair request and asked the tenant to contact them in writing at her earliest convenience for follow-up.

The tenant stopped paying rent and called Fair Housing in hopes it would persuade the landlord not to pursue an eviction. Once Fair Housing heard management's side and saw they had supporting documentation, they re-contacted the tenant. The tenant admitted she was behind in her rent, had received management's letter, acknowledged being contacted by maintenance and confessed to not responding or cooperating. She also verified her daughter was home alone and had just come out of the shower when the maintenance workers arrived for the initially scheduled repair appointment. Fair Housing dropped the matter and saw no reason for further action.

Why I believe the complaint was deemed unfounded by Fair Housing:

- The company kept good records that provided a reliable account of what occurred
- Management showed they were not trying to avoid their responsibilities
- Both maintenance and management's actions were reasonable
- The professionals made good faith efforts to address the repair in a timely manner
- The workers behaved appropriately and followed written policy
- The procedure maintenance adhered to was in the best interest of all involved

A vendor who follows proper protocol and does not require a lot of supervision or to be repeatedly told what is needed of him or her are sought after workers in this business.

ROLE-PLAYING SCENARIOS

A Learning Stage 67 – Occupancy Standards

Scenario:

These are three separate situations at the same rental property.

~ Situation 1 ~

Decoy1: "My family and I are interested in renting your two bedroom apartment."

Landlord: "How many occupants are in your family?"

Decoy1: "There are six of us all together."

Landlord: "Okay, here's an application. Be sure to read the attached procedures and criteria.

~ Situation 2 ~

Decoy1: "My family and I are interested in renting your two bedroom apartment."

Manager1: "How many are there in your family?"

Decoy1: "There are two adults and four children. Why?"

Manager1: "Because we have a 2+1 occupancy standard."

Decoy1: "What does that mean?"

Manager1: "It means that only 5 people are allowed to occupy that apartment."

Decoy1: "Does this mean we can't apply?"

Manager1: "No. If I were you I would still submit an application. I'll put a notation on your application that three of your children are very small and wouldn't take up that much space."

~ Situation 3 ~

Decoy2: "My family and I are interested in renting your two bedroom apartment."

Manager2: "How many occupants will there be?"

Decoy2: "There are a total of six of us. May I have an application please?"

Manager2: "You don't qualify."

Decoy2: "Why?"

Manager2: "We subscribe to a 2+1 occupancy standard. That means no more than five people may reside in that apartment."

Decoy2: "I would still like to have an application."

Manager2: "I'm sorry but we're out."

After the second set of decoys left, manager2 was seen giving out applications to other applicants. When manager2 was asked why she denied the decoy2 family an application, she gave the following explanation. "All six of them were big and tall. Can you imagine the wear and tear? Each one of them was the size of two people so I equated it to a family of twelve applying for occupancy."

Discussion Questions:

1. Write an evaluation on the landlord and the two managers

2. Were there any violations of Fair Housing laws?
3. Is it a law that there can be no more than two people per bedroom?
4. According to the 2+1 rule how many occupants may reside in a four bedroom apartment?

Follow-up Suggestions:

- Do not stray from your written policies and criteria
- Be certain that if you make a variance from your rules, it is an act allowable by law

Just for Fun:

A group of tourists were in Europe being led through an ancient castle.

Guide: "This place is 600 years old. Not a single stone in this castle has been touched. Not one thing has been altered, and nothing replaced in all that time."

Sightseer: "Well, they must have the same landlord I have."

*　　*　　*

Question: What do landlords do for fun?
Answer: Who knows? I haven't seen mine in the past 8 months.

*　　*　　*

For whosoever shall keep the whole law, and yet offend in one [point], he is guilty of all.

James 2:10 KJV

A Learning Stage 68 – Good Employee

If you handle each tenant the same per your policies, there is less room for discrimination claims. Follow and incorporate rules that are both legal and in line with enforcing agencies.

Remember the only information you can consider as factual, is what has been verified and supported by documentation.

Scenario:

A manager is following up with her supervisor regarding the processing of a prospective tenant's application.

Manager: "I confirmed that she has worked for that company for three years."
Supervisor: "How do you know that for certain?"
Manager: "The applicant, Sue told me."
Supervisor: "Did you contact the company?"
Manager: "Yes."
Supervisor: "Did they give you documentation of her employment?"
Manager: "No, but I called and spoke with them."

Supervisor: "Is this from a phone number that she gave you? Or did you obtain it from the phone book or look up the company's name online?"
Manager: "It was the number she wrote down on her application."
Supervisor: "How do you know that number doesn't belong to a friend of hers?"
Manager: "I don't."
Supervisor: "Right. Sounds like you need to call back and do more checking, Allie."

Allie believed this was a waste of her time, but she called the number listed on Sue's application for Sue's employer.

Manager: "Hello, I called earlier about Sue Happy."
Woman: "Oh yeah? Well, if you talked to someone about Sue, it must've been with my daughter, Leah. Leah! Get your butt in here the phone is for you. I told you it would be. Tell your kid to turn that television down; I can barely hear the lady."
Reference: "Who's this?"
Manager: "This is Allie. We spoke earlier about Miss Happy."
Reference: "Yeah, right. I mean, yes, Miss Happy is a responsible tenant."
Manager: "Really? How do you know Miss Happy?"
Reference: "She's been renting from us for some time now."
Manager: "She has? Have there ever been any NSF's?"
Reference: "Uh, what's that? She has been a good renter and we're sorry she's leaving."
Manager: "Okay. Thank you for your time."

Allie looked up the company name in the telephone book and online and found that the numbers matched each other, but was not the number Sue wrote on her application. Her supervisor walked into the room and saw her working.

Manager: "You may have been right about how to verify information. I just called the number Sue listed as her employer and I got someone's residence. When the reference came to the phone, she presented herself as the applicant's current landlord. Her voice is also identical to the voice of the current landlord I spoke to but with a different number."

Supervisor: "Wait awhile and call the number back and see who she claims to be then."

Allie called back, and the reference seemed more guarded this time.

Manager: "Hi, would you please verify your address with me."

Reference: "Uh, it's uh, I have to call you back."

Manager: "No. if you hang up without answering my question correctly I will deny the application."

Reference: "Okay, I don't have the address at the moment."

Manager: "Aren't you in the building right now?"

Reference: "Uh, yes. I mean, no. Listen, she is a good employee, and I recommend you hire her for the job. She's a good worker, a very hard worker."

Manager: "You know I just realized your voice sounds just like her current landlord's."

The manager used another line and called the phone number listed on the application for the prospect's current landlord. She heard the phone ring in the background and the rings were in sync with the rings on her end of the line. The manager hung up, and the phone stopped ringing in the background. She called back a second time and the phone again rang in sync with the ringing on her end of the line.

Discussion Questions:

1. Was the supervisor being too strict?
2. What are the pros to verifying the telephone number is a valid one?
3. By using the correct number from other legitimate resources, what could it reveal?
4. Did the manager or supervisor commit any Fair Housing violations? Explain.
5. List all the ways one may properly verify an applicant's employment?
6. What could prevent this confusion and encourage uniformity?
7. Now what should the manager do?

Follow-up Suggestions:

- Always document when calls were made, to whom, what was said, who you spoke with, and whether you left a message.
- Ask references to verify information with you that they should know.
- Wait awhile and call the number back and see if the same person answers.

Just for Fun

On December 23rd, Santa Claus, a generous landlord, noble lawyer and optimistic tenant, rode on the same elevator at a luxurious hotel. When the doors opened, they simultaneously spotted a $1000 bill on the floor. Which person picked up the bill?

Answer: Santa, because the others don't exist.

*   *   *

Q: How are a lawyer and a leech different?
A: When you die, a leech will stop sucking your blood and drop off.

*   *   *

Q: What distinction is there between a lawyer and an angry rhinoceros?
A: The lawyer charges more.

*   *   *

Where no counsel is, the people fall: but in the multitude of counsellors there is safety.
Proverbs 11:14 KJV

A Learning Stage 69 – Give & Take Judgments

Scenario:

A tenant telephoned the management company for her rental after making a gruesome discovery.

Tenant: "Hi, I'm calling because I found evidence that there are rodents in my home."

Manager1: "Yeah, we never had a report of that problem there before. You just moved in and now there are rodents? What do you want me to do about it?"

The tenant went to a hardware store and purchased a device that claimed to scare all rodents away. It emitted an electrical current undetected by humans and non-harmful. She continued finding droppings after repeated daily cleaning for one week.

Tenant: "Hi, I'm calling again because my rental has mice."

Manager2: "You say you're calling *again*? Who did you talk to the first time? It doesn't matter you shouldn't keep calling. We have a policy that

requires you to put all your repair requests in writing."
Tenant: "I'm sorry. I didn't relate this to being a repair."

The tenant sent in a written request to have something done to exterminate the rodents. The letter was respectful and brief, and it was mailed out the same day she spoke with Manager2. Another week went by without a response and the droppings were multiplying each day after she would clean. She did not want to purchase or distribute poison nor snap traps in her home as she was afraid her children would be endangered by them and the uninvited intruders. She made another trip to the hardware store and purchased some glue traps.

Two weeks went by, and she heard nothing from anyone in management. The rodents had begun gnawing into her food and the glue traps appeared ineffective. She told a friend about the problem who told her she should move. She just had her address changed, and the move was a difficult one, she could not bear to move again so soon.

~ The tenant telephones management again ~
Tenant: "Hi, I'm calling to find out if you received my repair request?"
Manager3: "If you'll tell me your name and address I can check on that for you."
Tenant: "My name is Rare Goodie-Goodie, my address is 666 Rodents Lane."
Manager3: "Okay, I'll look into that. Now, when did you send in the repair request and what was it for?"
Tenant: "I sent the request in over 3 weeks ago and it was for a rodent problem."

Manager3: "Rodents? You have experienced a rodent problem for 3 weeks? I'm so sorry to hear that. That is not normally something that requires a form. We like to receive notification right away on matters like that to attack the problem immediately. Something like that requires immediate attention to prevent an infestation."

Tenant: "I called twice and spoke with two different managers there and it was the second one who told me this was considered a repair and that I should make a written repair request, so that's what I did."

Manager3: "I apologize for the inconvenience and confusion. I'm going to call an exterminator right away and see how soon they can go out there. I'll call you back."

Manager3 called an exterminator that promised same day service and coordinated a time for them to respond that was convenient for the tenant. The exterminator company called back with their assessment and to acquire authorization for billing.

The tenant, exterminator, and Manager3 were clear that to completely eradicate the problem may require a series of traps before it was resolved. To expect an overnight fix would be impractical and unrealistic.

It appeared the unwelcomed guests were opportunist that had possibly entered when the doors were left wide open from workers preparing the rental for tenancy. The property no longer experienced the problem the remainder of this tenant's occupancy.

Manager3 acquired an estimate from the tenant of food she had to replace that had been contaminated, and the devices she purchased out of pocket to try to remedy the problem herself, along with a maid service to clean the place once the problem was solved and charged the owners of the property under a notation for "exterminator bill."

Discussion Questions:

1. Evaluate all three managers' performances. Which ones are valuable employees?
2. Which of the three managers would you want working for you and why? Explain.
3. If you were the manager how would you have handled the situation?
4. Did any of these managers violate your company policies? Explain.
5. Is customer service truly that important, as long as the problem is acknowledged and addressed?
6. What are key duties you require of your staff that these managers were lacking in?
7. Where did each of the managers err, and what things did they do right?
8. Whom might you strongly reprimand or write up for their behavior?
9. Is there any training you believe is appropriate for all 3 managers? Explain in detail.

Follow-up Suggestions:

- Have a repair policy that requires tenants to request non-emergent repairs in writing

- Ensure both tenants and staff understand what is constituted or considered as emergency repairs and how to report them consistently
- Have a designated person assigned to the property so tenants and owners know who to deal with primarily on matters as this. Such person should be knowledgeable and informed
- Treat clients as you would want to be treated: with respect and compassion
- Consider your customers' inconveniences and compensate them when warranted
- Sometimes you may have to take a financial hit to keep clients happy: however, don't be generous with owners' finances without their consent

Just for Fun:

Q: What's black and brown and looks good on an attorney?
A: A Doberman pinscher.

        *   *   *

Q: What's the difference between a porcupine and a Mercedes Benz full of lawyers?
A: The porcupine has pricks on the outside.

        *   *   *

(2) And the spirit of the LORD shall rest upon him, the spirit of wisdom and understanding, the spirit of counsel and might, the spirit of knowledge and of the fear of the LORD;
(3) And shall make him of quick understanding in the fear of the LORD: and he shall not judge after the sight of his eyes, neither reprove after the hearing of his ears:

(4) But with righteousness shall he judge the poor, and reprove with equity for the meek of the earth: and he shall smite the earth with the rod of his mouth, and with the breath of his lips shall he slay the wicked. (5) And righteousness shall be the girdle of his loins, and faithfulness the girdle of his reins.

Isaiah 11:2-5 KJV

A Learning Stage 70 – 3 Landlords Lose 3-Day Notice Cases

<u>Scenario</u>:

These are three court cases in which the landlords did not fare well. See if you can figure out why.

~ Case #1 ~

Landlord: "Your honor, I'm asking for possession of the premises and $200.00 for unpaid rent. I'll pass up my records to show the delinquency and notices the tenant was sent."

Judge: "I've reviewed the documents. Now, what do you have to say in your defense?"

Tenant: "I paid my full rent every month."

Landlord: "No, actually you got behind after the second month. You stopped paying on time."

Tenant: "My rent was $500 a month. You will see that in the 6 months I have lived on the property, I have paid $3,000 total plus another $600 security deposit. So I am not behind. Each month's check cashed by my landlord has the month written in the memo line."

Landlord: "Perhaps, but you got behind when you started paying late."

Tenant: "When is late exactly? You accepted my checks and cashed them which meant you acknowledged the terms that it was payment for rent for that month. Your 3 day notice is thus inaccurate as my rent was fully paid and accepted by you."

Landlord: "Wait a minute."

Judge: "I'm afraid your tenant is correct. There is proof of six months of tenancy and six months' worth of rent checks for the full $500 that you cashed. Case dismissed."

~ Case #2 ~

Tenant: "I know it's probably too late because we are to be in court on Monday, but if I can pay you money by Friday will you call off the eviction?"

Landlord: "You'd have to follow through."

Tenant: "I will. I promise."

Friday, that evening, the tenant personally handed the landlord a check for $300 of the $2,500 the landlord was demanding.

Monday, nothing changed in the landlord's mind so the case was pursued.

Tenant: "Your honor the landlord agreed to give me more time if I gave him a payment on Friday, which I did. He accepted the partial payment and I don't understand why we're here."

Landlord: "He said he'd pay the full $2500 on Friday and

if he did then he would not have to appear in court today."

Judge: "So then you did in fact agree to give him more time and enter into another agreement with him."

Landlord: "Yes."

Judge: "Then you nullified this 3-Day Notice and I have to dismiss the case."

Landlord: "Wait, no! You see he didn't honor his end to pay the full amount owed."

Judge: "Then you should not have accepted a partial payment, nor made a new agreement without issuing a new 3-Day Notice outlining the new terms. Case dismissed."

~ Case #3 ~

Judge: "Okay, I have reviewed the paperwork and everything appears to be in order. The proper notices were served and I find the proof of service is valid. What is your defense?"

Tenant: "The amount is not accurate on the 3-Day Notice and I understand it may not be overstated or it is rendered invalid."

Judge: "Why do you believe it is an overstated amount?"

Tenant: "Because they accepted a partial payment after they filed the case with the court and the payment is not credited to the amount they're suing me for."

Landlord: "That's impossible. We know not to accept payment without adjusting the amount and issuing a new 3-Day Notice. Our policy is to not accept partial payments of any kind."

Judge: "He disputes receiving and accepting payment, do you have proof otherwise?"

The tenant passed up a sheet of paper. The judge looked it over and had the bailiff show it to the plaintiff. The plaintiff confirmed the account number belonged to him.

Landlord: "We tried an automatic deposit program where tenants could make payments into our account online. It didn't work out so we discontinued it. Apparently that is how he was able to post that payment. But we did not knowingly accept that payment for a measly dollar. Therefore, that should not count."

Judge: "This bank statement shows a deposit of one dollar into your account after the 3 Day Notice was filed. Case dismissed."

Discussion Questions:

1. Explain why all three landlords' cases were dismissed by the judges in detail.
2. What mistakes did these landlords make?
3. What, if anything, did the landlords do right?
4. Do you believe the judges ruled incorrectly in any of the cases? Explain.
5. Is the burden of proving your case as a landlord equal to or greater than that of a tenant? Explain.
6. At your company, would any of these landlords have violated your policies? Explain.

Follow-up Suggestions:

Beware, Legal Aid and tenant attorneys are soliciting tenants with stall tactics in the courtroom. Many irresponsible tenants would rather pay an attorney to find a loophole to get them out of paying their debts. Do not make it easy for them to abscond from their responsibilities.

- Bring a cohesive file of pertinent evidence and Documentation to support your case.
- Make sure the court has a valid Proof of Service notice.
- If you decide to accept a partial payment make sure you update the amount you are seeking.
- Double check the amount being sought to be certain it is not overstated and exact.

Just for Fun:

Description of a very telling cartoon:
It depicts two people fighting over a cow. One is pulling the cow by the tail in one direction; the other person is pulling the cow in the opposite direction by the horns. Underneath you find a lawyer milking the cow.

* As long as you and your tenants persist on quarreling, neither one of you will get what you want. A third party, however, will insure they benefit and can do so without having to resolve your dispute.

*   *   *

In meekness instructing those that oppose themselves; if God peradventure will give them repentance to the acknowledging of the truth;
2 Timothy 2:25 KJV
And that they may recover themselves out of the snare of the devil, who are taken captive by him at his will.
2 Timothy 2:26 KJV

My brethren, be not many masters, knowing that we shall receive the greater condemnation.

James 3:1 KJV

A Learning Stage 71 – Fair Housing Rules

If you plan on being in the rental industry for any length of time, chances are you will have an interaction with the Department of Fair and Employment Housing (DFEH).

<u>Scenario</u>:

The Department of Fair Employment and Housing send out operatives called "testers" or "secret shoppers" to investigate complaints. Normally, if you are receiving a call from them, they may have already *shopped* you and are now giving you an opportunity to give your side. Review the below scenarios and evaluate the landlords' responses.

DFEH: "Yes, hello. I'm following up on a complaint of discrimination. I notice you don't have the posted signs present in your office. May I have a copy of your Application Procedure and Criteria?"

LL1: "Okay, I tell everybody that the rules are..."

DFEH: "No, I'm not asking you to tell me. I'd like to see them please."

LL1: "I don't have time to write that all down."

*

DFEH: "Yes, hello. I'm following up on a complaint of discrimination. Could you please give me your side of the call made by applicant Sue Happy please?"

LL2: "Oh her, she never called me."

DFEH: "I see. Well, are you sure? Would you like to check your records first?"

LL2: "No. I don't need to. She never called. (pause) Besides, we don't log in every call that comes in here."

*

DFEH: "Yes, hello. I'm following up on a complaint of discrimination. A Mister Vic Tim said you asked him how many children he had."

LL3: "Yeah, so what?"

DFEH: "You can't do that. That's a violation."

LL3: "What, that's crazy. I didn't do that. But if I ever decided to in the future, isn't it my right to know how many of those noisy brats a tenant is trying to intrude on my rental?"

*

DFEH: "Yes, hello. I'm following up on a complaint of discrimination from a Miss Honest Little. Can you tell me your version of your dealings with her?"

LL4: "What's her name? Ornery? Nope, I never met her."

DFEH: "Her notes say that on January 12th at 9 AM she spoke with you and set up a meeting for her to see the vacancy. She met with you on the 13th and you said she looked Indian and couldn't rent to her because she might scare the other residents."

LL4: "I never said that! In fact if I would've said anything to her, I would have been accommodating and let her know about the mosque two blocks over. Or I would have let her know about the vacancies and all the other Indians that live down the street in the Cool Complex, they have vacancies there too you know."

DFEH: "She remembers you very well."

LL4: "Well I don't remember her. January was four months ago. How am I supposed to remember everyone I saw, what I said, and what I did?"

DFEH: "She gave us a copy of the ad you placed, her phone bill with your number on it and an approximate 5-minute conversation."

LL4: "Well, I still say she's lying. I don't know her. I never spoke with her or met her."

*

DFEH: "Yes, hello. I'm following up on a complaint of discrimination. Do you accept children there?"

LL5: "Sometimes we do. It depends."

DFEH: "On what?"

LL5: "Depends on who's asking, how many kids it is, the ages, how many fathers are involved, if they're well behaved and clean, if the parents have good paying jobs and aren't on welfare. You know there are a lot of factors we consider. So sometimes we accept them and sometimes we don't."

DFEH: "Okay, I think we've heard enough."

LL5: "Oh, one final thing. Of course, they have to be legal citizens."

DFEH: "Why?"

LL5: "Because we're proud Americans and we know the city doesn't want us renting to *illegals*. You said you're from the city right?"

DFEH: "No, I'm from the Department of Fair and Employment Housing."

LL5: "Oh, you're with those guys? Never mind, I have to change my answer. Yes, we accept all children. But they must be accompanied at all times by a parent or guardian when walking through the complex. They can never be unattended for any reason."

Discussion Questions:

1. Evaluate all five landlords above from a scale of one to ten, ten being best.
2. Did any of the five landlords violate Fair Housing rules or any laws? Explain.
3. In the five encounters, would you have given different replies? If so, write down what you would have said differently.
4. When Fair Housing investigators call landlords, do they always identify themselves? Why or why not?
5. What statements, if any, were made by the landlords that accidentally gave more credibility to complaining applicants and surrendered power from the landlord?
6. What was said by the landlords in their defense that made them look even worse?

Follow-up Suggestions:

- If you routinely operate good business practices you will not need to rely on your memory
- Treat every caller and potential tenant who wants to view your vacancies as if they are a tester evaluating your performance

- Any-time you have a question about the law, consult a qualified attorney
- Attend Fair Housing workshops that provide attendees with handouts, they are beneficial and give people reading materials to refer to as resources at a later time

Some are so fearful of saying the wrong thing or asking the wrong question, it impedes their ability to do business. The best way to pacify this stress is to attend Fair Housing training as often as you can until you are comfortable you know the parameters. By knowing and following the law, you will no longer try to cater your answers to what you believe a possible Fair Housing operative wants to hear. Your answers and responses will be consistent and that should provide you with much relief.

Just for Fun:

Q: What do you call 5000 dead lawyers at the bottom of the ocean?
A: A good start!

    *   *   *

A manager is showing a couple around one of his vacant apartments. The husband looked up and said, "Hey! Wait a minute. Look, this apartment doesn't have a ceiling." The manager replied, "No problem…The people upstairs don't walk around that much."

    *   *   *

Question: If you are stranded on a desert island with a lion, a rattlesnake, and a lawyer, and you have a gun with only two bullets, what do you do?

Answer: Shoot the lawyer, twice.

*   *   *

Question: How can you tell when a lawyer is lying?
Answer: His lips are moving.

*   *   *

Get wisdom, get understanding: forget it not; neither decline from the words of my mouth.

Proverbs 4:5 KJV

Wisdom is the principal thing; therefore get wisdom: and with all thy getting get understanding.

Proverbs 4:7 KJV

How much better is it to get wisdom than gold! and to get understanding rather to be chosen than silver!

Proverbs 16:16 KJV

Wherefore is there a price in the hand of a fool to get wisdom, seeing he hath no heart to it?

Proverbs 17:16 KJV

A Learning Stage 72 – Maddie

I was visiting Maddie, a long-time friend, who has been a rental property owner for decades. I was about to leave when she asked me to stay a little while longer and sit in on an appointment she had with a potential applicant. Thirsty for any experience I could glean from, I chose to observe.

Maddie interviewed Khalia, an applicant, who responded to Maddie's ad.

Maddie: "So how old are you, hon'?"

Khalia: "Uh, thirty-nine. But what does that have…"

Maddie: "I see. Are you married?"

Khalia: "Well, no."

Maddie: "I go to Holy Jump Missionary. Do you attend church on a regular basis, hon'?"

Khalia: "No Ma'am. I used to attend now and then when my children were first baptized."

Maddie: "That's nice, you have children? I thought you said you were not married. How many children do you have?"

Khalia: "I have six altogether."

Maddie: "Six, my goodness! That's too many children. I know of no place that can accommodate so many youngsters."

Khalia: "Oh but not all of them live with me. Two are adults and one is about to enter into the military."

Maddie: "Well what are the ages of the children who will be living with you? And what are your childcare arrangements when you're at work? Children are not allowed to roam the neighborhood unaccompanied, hon'."

Khalia: "My children are ages 13, 10 and 6, and they're quite capable of looking after themselves when I'm not there. They're very well behaved and they aren't unruly."

Maddie: "That may be, but I promised the neighbors that I wouldn't put the wrong people in my rental. They're mostly retired people like me, and they like it quiet. No baseball games in the street, as that can lead to broken windows and damaged property."

Khalia: "They need to be allowed to go outside and play nearby, Ma'am."

Maddie: "Not there, hon', the neighbors will call me every few minutes to complain. Listen why don't you go through that door there and fix yourself something to eat. I would do it myself, but I'm practically crippled. I don't get around so good any more. I can't drive because my eyesight is so bad. I'm old, hon', and I live alone. That's why I had you meet me here at my house and not at the rental."

Khalia: "I'm fine. I'll pick up something after I leave here. You were going to give me the key to the house so I could see the inside."

Maddie: "Right. It's in my purse over there next to you, hon'. Would you hand it to me?"

Stella: "Key? Excuse me, but before you talk about keys,

did she complete an application and screening? Has she provided a deposit?"

Maddie: "Oh my, I forgot all about that. Here's the application for you to fill out."

Khalia: "I can't do that now I didn't bring my glasses. Why don't you fill it in for me?"

Maddie: "I told you, hon', my eyesight is so bad I can't drive and I have arthritis too."

Stella: "Maddie, the applicant needs to complete the application herself there's no way around that. Perhaps she should not have a key until she has provided a completed application and deposit."

Khalia: "Money, yes about that, I wasn't able to bring it all with me. I had to pay a friend of mine to let me use his car to drive out to your house to get the key and meet you. It's nearly an hour drive and I need gas money. But I can give you the deposit next week when I get paid again. The place sounds so wonderful. All my children are so excited they can't wait to move in."

Maddie asked what I thought, and I was candid. I strongly recommended she not accept any money, and not hand over keys until a credit and criminal background check was run which Khalia must pay for when a completed application was submitted. I also recommended she not ask any personal questions until she attended Fair Housing workshops and became acclimated with the laws.

Maddie's thinking was, "I've been doing this more years than you've been alive. I've always had personal sit-downs with all my renters over a nice meal to get acquainted with them to determine if they're good people. It's my property and I see nothing wrong with knowing more about them and their lifestyle, and giving them advice as well. I want us to be one happy family. It's how I've always handled the business."

Against my recommendation, Maddie gave Khalia the key to the residence. Khalia drove straight to the property, and she, her children, and boyfriend immediately moved in. The money Khalia gave Maddie was the only money Maddie received. Approximately one year later Khalia and her unauthorized occupants cost Maddie over $50,000 in lost rental income, to repair the damage they caused to the property, and in legal fees to ultimately evict. The non-financial costs were measured by the loss of lots of time, stress, peace of mind, and trips to court and her attorney's office in the jurisdiction of the rental property.

Discussion Questions:

1. Was anything Maddie said or did in violation of Fair Housing laws? Explain.
2. Do you have a procedure you follow interviewing prospective tenants? What is it?
3. Did Maddie do or say things that put her personal safety at risk? Explain.
4. What personal information did Maddie share, and invitations did she give, that could open the door for a tenant to take advantage of her as a landlord?

Follow-up Suggestions:

- Allow the application to ask most of the questions you need to know
- The Application Procedure (AP) and Resident Selection Criteria (RSC) should clearly outline the guidelines you use to accept and deny prospects
- Maddie could have avoided committing Fair Housing violations by allowing the application to pose proper legal questions relevant to the process
- The AP would have disqualified Khalia and explained a completed application was required to proceed
- Credit and criminal background checks should be mandatory for all applicants
- If the screening fee is not affordable, the application is not complete, the deposit is not paid, then keys and access to the rental ought to be denied

Just for Fun:

No application & No money = No keys & no entry!

*   *   *

Question: What's the difference between a dead skunk in the road and a dead lawyer in the road?
Answer: There are skid marks in front of the skunk.

*   *   *

Question: Why did God make snakes just before lawyers?
Answer: To practice.

*   *   *

Question: What's the definition of a lawyer?
Answer: A mouth with a life support system.

*   *   *

Question: What do you get when you cross a lawyer with a demon from hell?
Answer: No changes occur.

*   *   *

Question: Why is going to a meeting of the Bar Association like going into a bait shop?
Answer: Because of the abundance of suckers, leeches, maggots and nightcrawlers.

*   *   *

But he giveth more grace. Wherefore he saith, God resisteth the proud, but giveth grace unto the humble.
James 4:6 KJV

A Learning Stage 73 – Maintain a Balance

Scenario:

A woman in search of a new apartment noticed a man in uniform and stopped him for assistance.

Melissa: "Hi. Do you work here?"

Marvin: "Yes, I'm the maintenance supervisor."

Melissa: "I've been walking around here lost trying to find apartments 7C, 23D, and 1G."

Marvin: "I've got keys; I suppose I could let you in. But I think it's best if you go to the manager's office and let them show you those apartments."

Melissa: "I just came from there. There are two managers there and one is busy with a client. The other one said she was on her way out so she gave me these apartment numbers to find and look on my own."

Marvin: "Oh, then they're probably unlocked. But I'll go with you just in case."

Melissa: "Great. I appreciate that. I am pressed for time I have only a few minutes left before I have to go pick up my children."

Marvin: "How many kids do you have?"

Melissa: "Six."

Marvin: "Six? Wow! How old are you? You look too

young to have six children."

Melissa: "Three are mine, and the other three are special needs children I've adopted."

Marvin: "That's a nice thing." (pause) "You seem like a nice lady. I gotta be honest with you you'll never get accepted with that many kids. The largest apartment they have is a 3 bedroom and it's not big enough for a family of your size. Did you tell them you had six kids?"

Melissa: "No, and they didn't ask."

Marvin: "I guess not because two of those vacant apartments you wanted to see are on the second floor. They won't put any kids in upstairs apartments just for safety reasons. You know I have a friend who works at the Loco Lovers Vista two blocks over."

Melissa: "I know where that is."

Marvin: "They have vacancies over there. They also take anybody who can pay. I think you would feel more comfortable over there. It's also a more kid friendly environment. I suggest you go there. It's probably more in your price range too."

Manager1: "Oh good you're still here. I caught you."

Melissa: "I was just about to leave; your maintenance supervisor was just telling me that I don't qualify for an apartment here."

Manager1: "Oh? Why is that?"

Melissa: "Because he says I have too many children."

Marvin: "She has six children."

Manager1: "Thank you, Marvin, but I'll take it from here. Come find me later so we can have a chat please."

Marvin walked away, and Manager1 directed her attention back on Melissa.

Manager1: "I apologize for any misunderstanding. I would be happy to show you all the vacancies you believe suit your housing needs."

Melissa: "I've run out of time. I have to go pick up my children. Besides that, I don't want to waste my time looking if I'm just going to get denied."

Manager1: "I'm sorry you didn't get to see the apartments, but you are welcome to come back when you have more time or call and schedule an appointment. Let me provide you with an application and a copy of our criteria should you decide to apply."

Melissa: "Okay, thank you."

Melissa did complete and submitted an application. One week after the management received Melissa's paperwork, they met with a married couple with no children. They later accepted the couple as tenants. Melissa's calls and letters inquiring as to the status of her application were ignored.

Discussion Questions:

1. Should management be grateful Marvin took the time to show Melissa the vacancies?
2. Were there any Fair Housing violations committed? Explain.
3. Does Melissa have cause to claim discrimination? Explain.

<u>Follow-up Suggestions</u>:

- Train staff members to refer prospects to managers who are qualified to assist them
- Do not allow untrained staff to act outside of their training and job scope

<u>Just for Fun</u>:

Question: How many law professors does it take to change a light bulb?
Answer: You need 250 just to lobby for the research grant.

*   *   *

Question: What do you call a smiling, sober, courteous person at a bar association convention?
Answer: The caterer.

*   *   *

Wherefore, brethren, look ye out among you seven men of honest report, full of the Holy Ghost and wisdom, whom we may appoint over this business.
Acts 6:3 KJV
And if any man think that he knoweth any thing, he knoweth nothing yet as he ought to know.
I Corinthians 8:2 KJV
"So I have made you despised and humiliated in the eyes of all the people. For you have not obeyed me but have shown partiality in your interpretation of the law."
Malachi 2:9 NLT
Teach me, and I will hold my tongue: and cause me to understand wherein I have erred.
Job 6:24 KJV

A Learning Stage 74 – Special Accommodation

Scenario:

Paul reaches out to his friend, Jacob, who has helped him out in the past.

Paul: "I just accepted a tenant who now tells me he has a live-in aid. I'm going to reject him but thought I should bounce it off you before I do."

Jacob: "I'm glad you did. You've already accepted him so why would you now change your mind?"

Paul: "Because it's dishonest to tell me about another person, after the fact."

Jacob: "Ding! Violation! Strike One! That's not a viable reason to reject. He can use that to say you discriminated against him because you did not want to allow his accommodation and that's a Fair Housing violation."

Paul: "Okay, then if I reject the aid because it's a woman. Not to mention his girlfriend, who he's not married to. How do I know if she's a violent criminal? She has to fill out an application and complete the screening process just like all other tenants."

Jacob: "You have a problem, my friend. Pow, strike two. She is not a tenant. Your tenant is the guy renting from you not her. Pow, strike three, you're out. It is not your business what their sleeping or personal relationship is...you can't get into that."

Paul: "So how do I handle it?"

Jacob: "He must comply with the rules. Has he made an official request for an accommodation of having the live-in caretaker? It's preferred this request be made in writing, but many people don't know it's not mandatory. Don't you have a policy on this?"

Paul: "No."

Jacob: "Some reputable, reliable and verifiable medical, social worker, or professional must provide a written authorization for his caretaker. Then the key becomes this: is she doing her job? It's not about the fact she also happens to be his girlfriend, it's about is she providing the service of caretaker? At this stage, you have no legitimate reasons to deny him. If you were to use the reasons you've given me, you would have been in violation of discrimination by refusing to make accommodations and not even attempting to verify it."

Paul: "Alright I get it."

Jacob: "Oh and remember she's not a tenant, so she doesn't go through the applicant screening process. However, if you do a criminal check on all your applicants, you can require she provide the necessary information so one can be done on her as well. That is fair, reasonable and equal treatment. But she does not have to pay for that check, just like a person with a service animal does not pay a pet deposit."

Paul: "Alright, here we go. Equal treatment to me would mean she pays for the criminal check just like everybody else. Why should it have to come out of my pocket for *his* accommodation?"

Jacob: "For no other reason but to comply with the law. Remember my philosophy; don't whine about something unless you're willing to do something proactive to change it."

Discussion Questions:

1. Can a landlord reject a tenant for not disclosing the need for a live-in aid during the screening phase?
2. Is a landlord within his rights to reject a live-in aid if the aid also has a romantic relationship with the tenant? If the live-in aid is a relative can the landlord reject them? Explain.
3. Is the landlord allowed to probe the relationship between the tenant and live-in aid? If he/she finds out there is more to the relationship than a medical accommodation can the landlord reject the tenant? Explain.
4. Is a live-in aid required to complete an application and be screened just like a tenant? Explain.
5. Do you have a written policy that addresses how to handle these types of situations?
6. If you do a criminal check on everyone who resides in your rentals are you able to do one for a live-in aid? If you are, who pays for this?

Follow-up Suggestions:

- The rules that apply to live-in aids can be complex, and enforced differently by different housing agents. Speak with your local housing agency and acquire the rules that apply to disability accommodations
- For legal advice, speak with a qualified attorney before making a wrong decision
- If you are a member of an Apartment Association, call an advisor for advice and express any concerns you may have

Just for Fun:

Question: Why are lawyers like nuclear weapons?
Answer: When they land, they prevent anything from functioning for the next hundred years.

*   *   *

Question: Why are lawyers like nuclear weapons?
Answer: If one side has one, the other side has to get one.

*   *   *

Question: Why are lawyers like nuclear weapons?
Answer: Once launched, they can't be recalled.

*   *   *

Wherefore, my beloved brethren, let every man be swift to hear, slow to speak, slow to wrath:
James 1:19 KJV
But be ye doers of the word, and not hearers only, deceiving your own selves.
James 1:22 KJV

A Learning Stage 75 – The Answer to Church

Below are a variety of landlord responses to the same question.

~ Situation 1 ~

Prospect1: "Are there any churches in the area?"

Landlord1: "Yes. There's a Catholic church on Mission Street. I go there myself."

~ Situation 2 ~

Prospect2: "Are there any churches in the area?"

Landlord2: "Yes. What religion are you?"

Prospect2: "I'm a Charismatic."

Landlord2: "Are you really? I never understand you people. Seems like a bunch of nonsense to me. We're LDS."

Prospect2: "No kidding? Well, we never understood your religion."

~ Situation 3 ~

Prospect3: "Are there any churches in the area?"

Landlord3: "Yes. There are a variety to accommodate practically anyone."

Prospect3: "That sounds great. Any good temples nearby?"

Landlord3: "I cannot say whether any are good, bad or indifferent. I've passed a temple on Mission Street. You may want to drive the area, surf the internet or ask around to find what you're looking for."

~ Situation 4 ~

Prospect4: "Are there any churches in the area?"

Landlord4: "Yes."

Prospect4: "I'm looking for a good Lutheran church. Do you know of any?"

Landlord4: "No, not that are Lutheran. But I can refer you to a good church."

~ Situation 5 ~

Prospect5: "Are there any churches in the area?"

Landlord5: "No. The only thing we have around here are mosques. Oh, I'm sorry. That's the type of churches you people go to isn't it?"

~ Situation 6 ~

Prospect6: "Are there any churches in the area?"

Landlord6: "I can't discuss it. You must be a tester with Fair Housing setting me up."

~ Situation 7 ~

Prospect7: "Are there any churches in the area?"

Landlord7: "Practically on every corner. Which hypocritical faith do you ascribe to?"

Discussion Questions:

1. Write an evaluation for all seven landlords and how they answered the question.

2. What discrimination accusations can result from each situation?
3. How may this be addressed without opening yourself up to lawsuits?

Follow-up Suggestions:

- What religion the landlord is should not be voiced. It opens the door for problems:
  a. "You rejected my application because I'm a different religion than you are."
  b. "You denied us because we turned down your invitation to go to your church."
  c. Knowing where you fellowship, a disgruntled tenant may decide to wait in your church parking lot for you to report repairs on Sunday, in front of your pastor.
- Avoid controversial topics and stick to safe commentary about the property itself.

Just for Fun:

Question: How many lawyer jokes are there?
Answer: Just two, all the rest are true.

       *   *   *

Question: How many lawyers does it take to stop a moving bus?
Answer: Never enough.

       *   *   *

Question: Did you hear about the new microwave lawyer?
Answer: You spend eight minutes in his office and get billed as if you'd been there eight hours.

*   *   *

Question: What's the difference between a law firm and a circus?

Answer: At a circus, the clowns don't charge the public by the hour.

*   *   *

For there is no respect of persons with God.
Romans 2:11 KJV
And athletes cannot win the prize unless they follow the rules.
2 Timothy 2:5 NLT

A Learning Stage 76 – Child's Play

Whether in word or by one's behavior, biases have a way of seeping through the surface and revealing themselves.

<u>Scenario</u>:

Sorrowful: "Dude, this is Sorrowful, I'm Paul's niece. Dude, listen, I'm managing my grandfather's apartment complex. He has a vacancy, which is such a drag. He has had so many problems with parents and their children, so I suggested we put in the ad "no children" but my uncle Paul said we couldn't do that. My grandfather is cowering and said he wants to abide by the law, and if it's a violation, then I'm to give everybody an equal shot."

Jacob: "Don't ever single out children or any protected class in advertising. You must open that rental to everybody and give everyone a fair shake."

Sorrowful: "But Dude, children have always been a pain over here."

Jacob: "You cannot discriminate. And never target a protected class in writing."

~ One month later ~

Sorrowful: "Dude, we did what you said and unfortunately the most qualified was a single father with 3 kids. My grandfather said I should accept them, so I did. Dude, these kids are unruly, and they like to wrestle and throw balls at the walls keeping other tenants up. This goes on from about midnight and I have been getting complaints from others who want those *brats* gone too."

Jacob: "Notify the tenant that you have received noise complaints and ask him to cure the problem within 3 days."

~ One week later ~

Sorrowful: "Dude, I talked to the father last week, and I don't know what he did, but the problem stopped. Now we're getting complaints that these rowdy kids of his are playing ball in the common area. One tenant got struck in the head because these brats didn't have enough sense to stop tossing balls until people finished walking by."

Jacob: "Notify the tenant that there is a safety issue, and any activity that restricts safe access through the complex is prohibited."

~ One month later ~

Sorrowful: "Dude, I'm tired of dealing with these *brats*. The father stopped the kids from playing ball after I spoke with him. But for the past two weeks these *brats* have been skateboarding and riding their bikes in the driveway. When the other tenants try to enter, they don't move right away and have made them wait. I'm getting so many complaints on this it's pathetic."

Jacob: "Save all those complaints, keep documenting everything and send the tenant another letter, letting him know that skateboarding, bicycling, playing are not allowed in the driveway. It is also prohibited to impede and block vehicles from entering or exiting the premises."

Sorrowful: "Dude, I heard the dad lost his job too. He didn't pay this month's rent either. Should I send him an eviction notice with the letter about blocking the driveway?"

Jacob: "You could. I think I would give him two separate 3-Day Notices."

Sorrowful mailed the following letter to the tenant:

Taye Kadvantage
Dude, not only did you not pay your rent, but again I'm getting complaints about those kids of yours. The newest complaint is that they have been riding bikes and skateboards in the driveway and taking their time moving out of the way. Dude, don't you know children are not allowed to skateboard in the driveway?! If your rent is not received by June 10th we will start eviction proceedings.

Taye Kadvantage did not pay his rent and filed a discrimination lawsuit against Sorrowful and her grandfather.

Discussion Questions:

1. Would you have handled this the same way Sorrowful did? Explain.
2. What one word in Sorrowful's letter could cause her to lose her case against the tenant?
3. List things Sorrowful could have done to strengthen her actions to demonstrate she was not discriminating against the family because of the children.
4. Do you think Sorrowful would help or hurt her case if she were to explain the situation to a Fair Housing investigator? Explain.
5. Was there any important advice that Sorrowful was given that she did not follow?

Follow-up Suggestions:

- Have a complaint policy
- Require that residents put their grievances in writing
- Your rules should not single a group of people out and should apply to all equally
- Be cognizant of what you put in writing and send to tenants, as it cannot be changed later

Just for Fun:

Question: How many lawyers does it take to change a light bulb?
Answer: None, they'd rather keep their clients in the dark.

*   *   *

Question: How many law professors does it take to change a light bulb?

Answer: You need 250 just to lobby for the research grant.

*   *   *

Question: How many personal injury attorneys does it take to change a light bulb?

Answer: Three--one to turn the bulb, one to shake him off the ladder, and the third to sue the ladder company.

*   *   *

Q: How many lawyers does it take to screw in a light bulb?

A: One; the lawyer holds it while the rest of the world revolves around him.

*   *   *

Who is a wise man and endued with knowledge among you? let him shew out of a good conversation his works with meekness of wisdom.

James 3:13 KJV

A Learning Stage 77 – The Fill In

Management companies should have policies regarding the handling of applications for their employees to follow.

<u>Scenario</u>:

Messy Mary from Risky Business Management telephoned Mr. Leech, an applicant, for an update. "Mr. Leach? Good morning. I was calling to let you know that you are welcome to come back down to our office now. Your application is finished and ready for further processing. We only need you to come to our office at your earliest convenience to sign it."

~ One hour later Mr. Leech arrived at Risky Business Management ~

Manager: "Okay, Mr. Leech, my staff has rewritten your application for you since yours was not legible. Look it over and make sure it's all accurate."

Applicant: "No need. I trust you. What's the name of the person who wrote this in for me?"

Manager: "Connie."

Applicant: "Please tell Connie thank you. I see she has

real pretty and neat handwriting. I just sign here?"

Manager: "Yes."

Applicant: "Now where is the application I filled out?"

Manager: "It's in your file. But since we have the new one we can throw the old one out."

Applicant: "Why not just give it back to me. I'd feel better knowing I had it and that a paper with my personal information wasn't lying around somewhere accessible to some dumpster diver."

Manager: "We could also shred it for you before trashing it. We could do it now so you can see it being done."

Applicant: "Okay, yes let's do that. I'll feel more comfortable."

~ Six months later the boss has summoned the manager in to her office ~

Boss: "Have a seat. Do you remember Mr. Leech?"

Manager: "Yes, vaguely."

Boss: "He has filed a discrimination lawsuit against you. Now defend yourself."

Manager: "Here's all the information in his file. He initially turned in an illegible application, so we had to redo it for him, and have him come back in and sign it. Then we began processing the application and found he lied about several things. So we couldn't process it any longer. We tried calling and couldn't get him."

Boss: "Did you mail a rejection letter?"

Manager: "No, we called and asked him to call us back to tell him the status of his application but didn't hear back. Why?"

Boss: "He says he didn't lie on his application. He says you purposely wrote down wrong information to reject him."

Manager: "That's not true."

Boss: "Great, prove it. Let me see the original application he filled out in his own handwriting."

Manager: "I no longer have it. I shredded it."

Boss: "He says he has the original application, and he handed it over to Fair Housing."

Manager: "Really? I'm pretty sure; well I thought we shredded the original."

Boss: "He claims he asked for his original back, and you gave it to him."

Manager: "I do remember him asking for it back. Now I don't know for sure."

Boss: "Our policy says you are to maintain all documents until the whole file is destroyed. What does your notes indicate about what happened to the original?"

Manager: "Unfortunately, it doesn't. I made no notation about that."

Boss: "Do your notes state who filled out the application for him?"

Manager: "No. It might have been Ginger or Marge."

Boss: "It was Connie according to him, and she no longer works here. It's never good for an applicant to be a better record keeper, with a better memory than you."

Discussion Questions:

1. List all the reasons the manager will now have as a struggle proving Mr. Leech lied.

2. Is there ever a good reason to discard an original application? Explain why and why not.
3. Does the manager have anything in her favor to support her side?
4. Did the manager do anything right?
5. Was there anything the manager did wrong?
6. What would you do to prevent this problem from occurring to you? Explain in detail.
7. Who has a higher burden to prove themselves, the applicant or the manager? Why?

Follow-up Suggestions:

- Be a good example for your staff to emulate
- Have a policy for processing applications and teach your staff to be in compliance
- Discard files at a designated time that works best for you and your company
- Sending out rejection letters consistently can serve as good record keepers
- It is not wise for a staff member to complete any portion of one's application
- If you deviate from written policy, you start a new precedence for everyone

Just for Fun:

Q: What's the difference between a lawyer and a trampoline?
A: You take off your shoes before you jump on a trampoline.

* * *

Q: What's the difference between a lawyer and a terrorist?

A: You can negotiate with a terrorist.

*   *   *

Q: What do you get if you put 100 lawyers in your basement?
A: A whine cellar.

*   *   *

Q: What do you call a lawyer gone bad?
A: Your honor.

*   *   *

Thou hast rebuked the proud [that are] cursed, which do err from thy commandments.

Psalm 119:21 KJV

The proud have digged pits for me, which [are] not after thy law.

Psalm 119:85 KJV

Look not every man on his own things, but every man also on the things of others.

Philippians 2:4 KJV

A Learning Stage 78 – Couples of Options

As a landlord you have the ultimate say of who is permitted to move in to your rentals. However, if you violate the laws that govern you, you could lose that privilege.

<u>Scenario</u>:

Darby: "Hi, I'm Darby, and I emailed you to see your vacancies."

Landlord: "Right. My wife handles all that internet stuff. Are you wearing mascara?"

Darby: "Yes. Now, about those vacancies…You have five of them right?"

Landlord: "Yes. This one has brand new carpeting, new blinds and as you can see, it has a newly remodeled kitchen with new appliances and granite countertops."

Darby: "This is really nice."

Landlord: "It's a good size for a nice couple."

Darby: "Yes, if this represents what your other vacancies are like, my boyfriend and I will be very happy here. I can't wait to see the other vacancies."

Landlord: "Well, this is the only one available, and I do have applications in."

Darby: "Oh, I thought you said you have five vacancies. Well, then I better fill out an application now."

Landlord: "We're all out. You're welcome to check back in a couple of days and see if we have gotten any more applications in. Let me walk you out."

~ One hour later a married couple met with the landlord ~

Husband: "Hi, my wife emailed you to see your vacancies."

Landlord: "Right. We have five of them that would be perfect for a couple like you two. This first one has brand new carpeting, new blinds and as you can see, it has a newly remodeled kitchen with new appliances and granite countertops."

Husband: "Oh, honey, look at that kitchen. It's just perfect for you."

Landlord: "Do you still want to see the other four or would you like to fill out an application now?"

Husband: "Sure, let us see the other four."

The landlord was eager to show the couple all five vacancies and immediately offered them an application to complete.

Two days later, and every couple of days thereafter, Darby, contacted the landlord to see if he had any blank applications available. The landlord never had applications for Darby and his boyfriend, yet continued to give them out to all married or heterosexual couples.

Discussion Questions:

1. Did the landlord exhibit any behavior that is considered discriminatory? Explain.
2. What should the landlord have done differently?
3. When did the landlord's demeanor toward Darby shift?
4. Were there examples of preferential treatment exhibited by the landlord? Explain.

Follow-up Suggestions:

- When you know better, do better.

Just for Fun:

Question: What is a criminal lawyer?
Answer: Redundant.

*   *   *

Question: Why does California have the most attorneys, and New Jersey have the most toxic waste dumps?
Answer: New Jersey got first pick.

*   *   *

Question: What happened to the banker who went to law school?
Answer: Now she's a loan shark.

*   *   *

Question: Where do vampires learn to suck blood?
Answer: Law school.

*   *   *

Q: How was wire invented?
A: Two lawyers pulling on a penny.

*   *   *

But if ye have respect to persons, ye commit sin, and are convinced of the law as transgressors.

James 2:9 KJV

For if we sin wilfully after that we have received the knowledge of the truth, there remaineth no more sacrifice for sins,

Hebrews 10:26 KJV

A Learning Stage 79 – Nightmare Pets

Whether you allow pets or not, it is best to have some type of written policy in place regarding how you address the issue.

Scenario:

Caller1: "I'm calling about your one bedroom apartments, and I want to know if you accept pets."
Landlord: "No. This is a no pet building."
Caller1: "But my dog is very small. He's housebroken and very clean."
Landlord: "I'm sorry, but we do not accept any pets under any circumstances. Aside from that, you sound very young, how old are you?"
Caller1: "I'm 19, but I…"
Landlord: "Nineteen? No, I'm sorry. Good-bye."

~ Three hours later ~

Caller2: "Hi, I'm interested in seeing your vacant apartments, but I have a cat."
Landlord: "Well, we don't allow pets in the building."
Caller2: "My husband and I are both doctors, and the cat is very low maintenance."
Landlord: "Hmm, well you sound like responsible people, maybe I'll reconsider."

Caller2 was invited to come see the apartment, and the couple completed applications. They were later accepted as tenants. The landlord felt justified in his decision as the couple was older and in great paying professions should the cat cause damage. He asked them not to let anyone know he was bending the rules for them.

~ Six months later ~

The landlord noticed there was an increase in applicants with pets, and his vacancies were not being filled. He decided to adopt a new policy and told everyone who applied that he did accept applicants with pets. Shortly thereafter, he filled all his vacancies.

~ Four months later ~

The landlord decided to go back to a "no pet" policy and would no longer accept any new applicants with pets. This alteration was unbeknownst to Liz who called her friend and recommended the friend apply.

Liz: "Guess what. I've been living at the Nightmare Apartments for two months now and me and my Mastiff, Terror, have been very happy."

Caller1: "What? I applied there less than a year ago, and he said I couldn't even look at the vacant apartments because I had my little Chihuahua, Mousie."

Liz: "I'm sure it's not personal. Maybe he's had a change of heart. The apartment next to me just became available. The guy that lived there had a Mastiff, like me. He was a slob. I'm sure you'd get in because you and Mousie are so clean. Apply and I'll be a reference for you. They have a lot of cleaning to do in that apartment before it's ready, but get your application in before anybody else does and I'm sure it'll be yours."

~ Twenty minutes later ~

Caller1: "Hi, I'm interested in submitting an application for apartment 16B."

Landlord: "Come on down, it's not ready yet but will be in a few days."

~ One hour later ~

Caller1: "Hi, I'm the one who called about seeing apartment 16B."

Landlord: "Are you even old enough to rent an apartment? How old are you?"

Caller1: "I'm 20, yes I'm old enough. Oh, I also have a dog, that won't be a problem will it?"

Landlord: "Dog? Sorry, we don't allow pets in the building."

Caller1: "What? But I can see big dogs running around in those two apartments right there."

Landlord: "I don't care. I'm telling you, this is a 'no pet' building."

Caller1 filed a discrimination lawsuit against the landlord. She provided the dates of her interactions with the landlord and notes she had taken after each encounter. She gave Liz' contact information as a witness. Caller1 believes she was treated differently because she is Native American and because of her age.

Fair Housing had testers call and apply for the same vacancy. Later, the landlord was asked for his version of his encounters with Caller1 and initially said it never happened. Then the landlord said he deals with so many people and as such he did not remember anything about what he said, but proclaimed he treats everyone equally. He said that he did make a change some months back and began accepting tenants with pets, but it did not work out, so he switched back to being a no pet building. However, he could not recall the dates of when those changes were made and had no written procedures or criteria.

Discussion Questions:

1. Does Caller1 have a good case against the landlord? Explain.
2. What should the landlord have done differently? Explain.
3. What significant role could written criteria have played in this case? Explain.
4. Is it apparent that this landlord has certain biases that may get him in trouble? Explain.
5. Did everything the landlord said to Fair Housing in his defense help him? Explain.

Follow-up Suggestions:

- Take good notes
- If you are going to ask questions, have a set of questions to ask everyone
- Treat each person fairly

- Understand the importance of, and utilize, written guidelines and criteria
- When you make changes to your written policies always put the date of those modifications on the documents
- Avoid any dialogue that violates Fair Housing laws and stick to protected commentary

Just for Fun:

Judge: "You seem to be in some distress testifying. Is anything the matter?"

Witness: "Well, your Honor, I swore to tell the truth, the whole truth and nothing but the truth, but every time I try, some lawyer objects."

*   *   *

Reaching the end of a job interview, the Human Resources Officer asks a young engineer fresh out of the Massachusetts Institute of Technology a question.

H.R. Officer: "And what starting salary are you looking for?"

Engineer applicant: "In the region of $125,000 a year, depending on the benefits package."

H.R. Officer: "Well, what would you say to a package of five weeks' vacation, 14 paid holidays, full medical and dental, company matching retirement fund to 50% of your salary, and a company car leased every two years, say, a red Corvette?"

Engineer applicant: "Wow! Are you kidding?

H.R. Officer: Yes, but you started it."

*   *   *

But the wisdom that is from above is first pure, then peaceable, gentle, and easy to be entreated, full of mercy and good fruits, without partiality, and without hypocrisy.
James 3:17 KJV

A Learning Stage 80 – Passing the Buck

<u>Scenario</u>:

Buck, a tenant, contacts his management company to report a problem.

Tenant: "Hello, I live in condo 16, my name is Buck Pass. I might have fleas or something because I have all these red marks on my body. Can you send someone out?"

Manager1: "Yes, I'll send someone out right away."

~ Three days later ~

Tenant: "Hi, I called 3 days ago about possible fleas and no one has shown up yet."

Manager1: "Buck in apartment 16, right? That's a no pet building, get rid of the pet and we can send someone over to look into the fleas."

Tenant: "Pet? What pet? I don't have one and you said you'd send someone right away."

Manager1: "Okay, I'll call an exterminator."

The next day the tenant left a message that he was going to stay at a motel until the problem was fixed, and asked that management call him on his cell phone to keep him updated on when he could return.

After hearing nothing for two days, he began calling every hour from 8 A.M. to 5 P.M. and no one would answer the phone and speak with him. The next day he made a trip to management's office and he was told the manager for his rental was in the field and unavailable. They claimed Buck would have to wait for his manager to contact him.

The following day, management had an exterminator go out. The exterminator concluded that the condo had bedbugs not fleas. They bug bombed the place and told management the tenant was welcome to return.

Management sent the bill to the tenant and demanded payment. The tenant tried calling but never got his manager, and his calls were never returned. Shortly thereafter, the tenant continued experiencing a problem with these pests. He sent management a letter regarding how he did not feel it was his fault; he was not paying the bill, especially for a problem that was unresolved and still occurring.

Management called the property owners and the couple disagreed on how the bill should be handled so the manager decided to pursue the opinion that agreed with his. The only thing both owners did agree on was that the problem should be taken care of quickly so the bugs did not spread to others' units.

The exterminator company said it was not their fault the tenant was still claiming to have a bedbug problem. As they had done their job, either the tenants brought more bedbugs back in or the bedbugs from an adjacent attached condo was the source and bedbugs were returning to the tenant's condo through an adjoining wall the condos shared. They suggested the only way to cure the problem was to get the association involved to inspect the adjoining wall, poll the neighbors residing at the condo, and determine if others had the same problem to locate the source of the bedbugs.

The association manager said there had been no other reports of bedbugs but they would ask and distribute tips on how to avoid the problem and report it to them. However, they did nothing and took no action. Five more days had gone by. Buck again moved out of the rental and into a motel.

The manager for Buck's condo saw he was getting the runaround so he sent the association a letter explaining the circumstances and asking for their cooperation. No reply was sent, nor appeared to be forthcoming.

The owners went to the condos and spoke with as many of the other individual condo owners of that community they could to further investigate. They found that others had also had a bedbug problem that they reported to the association, yet no one would speak with them about it. Two owners pointed out the residence of a board member, but when the owners went to speak with him, there was no answer at the door. The couple wrote a note asking for the board member to contact them at his earliest convenience. A few days later the board member called and left a message blaring, "Listen, don't come to my home again bothering me on my time off. I don't appreciate you harassing me leaving notes on my door intruding on my personal time. Don't contact me again!"

The owners shared the message with their manager and asked him to do something about it. The manager said it was not his job to deal with the association and he had only contacted them as a courtesy. He recommended the owners deal with the association personally or hire legal counsel.

The manager told Buck he would not send an exterminator out again until he paid the first bill. He blamed Buck for the bedbugs. Buck was so frustrated he stopped paying rent and moved out of the condo after residing there fourteen years.

Discussion Questions:

1. Evaluate each of the parties involved and describe in detail if there were things they could have and should have done to improve the outcome.
2. Were those in authority fulfilling their duties? Explain.
3. Was this a bad tenant whom they should be glad to be rid of?
4. What should have been the primary focuses of all parties involved?
5. Who caused the problem?
6. How did each person's response contribute to a further dilemma?
7. What do you recommend the next steps should be to properly address the issue?

Suggestions:

- As owners, be aligned so you can provide a clear direction for your managers and agents to follow
- Board members who do not want the added responsibility should not take on the position and owner votes should reflect that

- Focus on exterminating the problem as quickly as possible, fault can be determined later
- Hire reputable exterminators who are experienced in treating Bedbugs, it's a specialty
- Treat others as you would like to be treated

Just for Fun:

When an employment application asks who is to be notified in case of emergency, I always write, "A very good doctor."

*   *   *

When my boss asked me who is the stupid one, me or him? I told him everyone knows he doesn't hire stupid people.

*   *   *

My job is secure. No one else wants it.

*   *   *

Do it tomorrow. You have made enough mistakes for today.

*   *   *

Woe unto them that decree unrighteous decrees, and that write grievousness [which] they have prescribed;
                                    Isaiah 10:1 KJV
Then said they, Come, and let us devise devices against Jeremiah; for the law shall not perish from the priest, nor counsel from the wise, nor the word from the prophet. Come, and let us smite him with the tongue, and let us not give heed to any of his words.
                                 Jeremiah 18:18 KJV
Childish leaders oppress my people, and women rule over them. O my people, your leaders mislead you; they

send you down the wrong road.
Isaiah 3:12 KJV
Therefore my people are gone into captivity, because [they have] no knowledge: and their honourable men [are] famished, and their multitude dried up with thirst.
Isaiah 5:13 KJV
Woe unto them that draw iniquity with cords of vanity, and sin as it were with a cart rope:
Isaiah 5:18 KJV
Woe unto them that call evil good, and good evil; that put darkness for light, and light for darkness; that put bitter for sweet, and sweet for bitter!
Isaiah 5:20 KJV
Woe unto [them that are] wise in their own eyes, and prudent in their own sight!
Isaiah 5:21 KJV

A Learning Stage 81 – Comparable Difference

Refrain from getting stuck in a rut. Be willing to compromise when the situation warrants it as a business person.

<u>Scenario</u>:

A landlord is about to deliver news to an applicant that he hopes will be beneficial to them both.

Landlord: "I'm pleased to tell you that you have been accepted as a tenant."
Tenant: "That's great."
Landlord: "There's just one other formality. Do you have any pets?"
Tenant: "No, not now, not ever."
Landlord: "Perfect. That's just what I want to hear. Just sign this lease and initial this line here that you do not have a pet and you understand this is a 'no pet' building."

~ Two months later ~

Tenant: "I'm here to drop off this doctor's authorization for my animal."

Landlord: "Animal? What are you talking about, I'm not reading that. You can't have any pets in this building. We discussed this. Do you want to review your signature on the documents that clearly stated this is a *no pet* building?"

Tenant: "No, no need."

~ One week later ~

Landlord: "What is this? Is that a Bulldog?"

Tenant: "Yes."

Landlord: "What's it doing here? I told you no pets, especially not one of those. Those things slobber all over the place. If I let you have that my insurance would be cancelled. Besides, you're in breach of your lease."

Tenant: "No. At the time I signed that lease I was fine. I later suffered some problems, and this Bulldog helps me with those issues."

Landlord: "That comment had more bull in it than your Bulldog. What problems did you suffer? If you can't prove to my satisfaction you need that Bulldog, you're out of here!"

Tenant: "I did what I'm supposed to do. I don't want to discuss it any further."

Landlord: "I can't agree with you more."

The landlord served the tenant notice to correct the violation by getting rid of the animal, or be evicted. The tenant refused to get rid of the dog and reported the incident to Fair Housing. He claimed he was being denied his request for a reasonable accommodation.

Fair Housing contacted the landlord who hung up on them and refused to speak to them. They sent the landlord a letter, and he hired an attorney.

Discussion Questions:

1. Will Fair Housing find the landlord in violation? Explain.
2. What evidence will the landlord use to defend his actions? Will it help his case?
3. Indicate what the tenant will present to prove his case against the landlord?
4. Was the landlord obligated to contact the doctor on the authorization note? Explain.
5. Should the landlord have handled this situation differently? Explain.

Just for Fun:

There was a lot of shouting going on in the court.
Judge: The next person in this court who dares to utter a word will be thrown out.
Defendant: Me, me!

*   *   *

In a criminal case, the defense counsel had just moved for continuance on the grounds that a defense witness was not present in court. The rest follows:
The Court: "Well why don't we call the list of witnesses and see who's here?"
[The list of witnesses was called in open court and the supposedly *absent* witness answered "Present"]

The Defense Attorney: "Your Honor, I move for continuance on the grounds of surprise. *He promised me he wouldn't be here.*"

*   *   *

He that despised Moses' law died without mercy under two or three witnesses:
Hebrews 10:28 KJV

A Learning Stage 82 – Accentuate the Positive

<u>Scenario</u>:

These three cases are what can occur when landlords and managers become relaxed and veer off the path of safe and protected commentary.

~ Case # 1 ~

Applicant1: "Hi. Thank you for agreeing to meet with me on such short notice."
Landlord: "No problem. I love your accent. Where are you from?"
Applicant1: "I was born in India, but I grew up in England."
Landlord: "I love hearing you talk, it's unusual to hear someone like you talk that way."

The landlord showed applicant1 all the vacant units and gave her an application. He rejected her application because she did not have six months local rental history and he feared she may not be a U.S. citizen.

~ Case # 2 ~

Applicant2 showed up for the apartment viewing seated in a wheelchair.

Applicant2: "Okay, so this downstairs apartment is the exact same floor plan as another upstairs apartment that you also have available right?"

Landlord: "Well, yes. But I think it best you stay on the bottom floor because how would you get up there? We don't have elevators you know."

Applicant2: "I don't like living on bottom floors. Would you consider installing an elevator or building a ramp?"

Landlord: "I'll mention it. But for now, how about you concentrate on the first floor."

The manager did not look into anything and denied the application believing to accept this tenant, would be a lawsuit waiting to happen.

~ Case # 3 ~

Applicant3: "I like the place, and you seem to like it too, so what's the problem?"

Tara: "Well, mom, we won't be able to get it unless we have a co-signor. Falco does not have enough income to support us yet, but he will. He's got a chance to get hired working for his uncle, and he has applications in all over town."

Applicant3: "No, I told you if you let him move back in with you again when they let him out, not to come to me for help."

Tara: "But mom, how can he do better if no one is willing to help? Give him a chance."

Applicant3: "How many chances do you think he should have? Look at how many you have already given him. You called me down here for this?"

Landlord: "Excuse me, I couldn't help but overhear your conversation. It sounds like your mother is trying to give you some good advice. Without a co-signor, we would have to reject you anyway because there's not enough income. I also didn't know Falco is just a boyfriend. You referred to him as your husband to us, because as we told you before, we prefer to rent to married, stable couples."

Tara: "Mom, if you don't co-sign, Falco will get mad. I don't need this right now, please."

Applicant3: "Okay, but this is really the last time."

Landlord: "Sounds like this 'Falco' has too many issues. No, this smells like domestic violence to me, and like the two of you would be a revolving door. We are looking for a more stable, older couple committed to each other. One who has a sense of family and old fashioned values. Although we have taken criminals before, if your boyfriend has been arrested we don't want him. He sounds like a repeat offender with a bad temper."

Tara: "What if we pay in cash? We can pay you two months in advance. Our current landlords are going to pay us some money our attorney says we're owed from them. And my mom says she'll co-sign for us. Then the child support payments should come in regularly for my kids."

Landlord: "Kids? I told you, no children allowed."

Tara: "I know, don't worry. They don't live with me, they live with my mother."

Landlord: "If they live with your mother, then that money should go to your mother. There are too many immoral shenanigans happening with you. If your income is not coming from a bonafide job, then I have to reject it as income. Sorry, no way can I accept you under these circumstances. You have to leave now, goodbye."

Discussion Questions:

1. Rate the landlords' performances in the 3 above cases and grade them on a scale of 1 to 10 with ten being best.
2. Were there any violations of your company policy made? Explain.
3. Did the landlords commit any Fair Housing violations? Explain.
4. Did the landlords have any legal reasons to deny the 3 different applicants? Explain.
5. What statements were made by the landlords that could give the applicants reasons to suspect their denials were based on discrimination?
6. How would you have handled the situations differently?
7. Do the legitimate reasons to deny an applicant override any and all Fair Housing violations a landlord commits? Explain.

Follow-up Suggestions:

- Be consistent
- Stick to commentary about the property and its amenities

- Have and supply your Application Procedure in writing to every interested applicant. It will help them self-qualify
- Avoid giving personal advice and interjecting your point of view in family disagreements
- Use valid legal reasons when denying applicants and concentrate solely on that

<u>Just for Fun:</u>

An independent woman started her own business. She was shrewd and diligent, so business kept coming in. She soon realized that she needed an in-house counsel, so she began interviewing young lawyers.

"As I'm sure you can understand," she started off with one of the first applicants, "in a business like this, our personal integrity must be beyond question."

She leaned forward and asked, "Mr. Peterson, are you an 'honest' lawyer?"

"Honest?" replied the job prospect. "Let me tell you something about honest. Why, I'm so honest that my dad lent me $15,000 for my education and I paid back every penny the minute I tried my very first case."

"Impressive. And what sort of case was that?"

"My dad sued me for the money."

*   *   *

I said, I will take heed to my ways, that I sin not with my tongue: I will keep my mouth with a bridle, while the wicked is before me.

Psalm 39:1 KJV

I was dumb with silence, I held my peace, even from good; and my sorrow was stirred.

Psalm 39:2 KJV

My heart was hot within me, while I was musing the fire burned: [then] spake I with my tongue,

Psalm 39:3 KJV

LORD, make me to know mine end, and the measure of my days, what it [is; that] I may know how frail I [am].

Psalm 39:4 KJV

Surely every man walketh in a vain shew: surely they are disquieted in vain: he heapeth up [riches], and knoweth not who shall gather them.

Psalm 39:6 KJV

Deliver me from all my transgressions: make me not the reproach of the foolish.

Psalm 39:8 KJV

I was dumb, I opened not my mouth; because thou didst it.

Psalm 39:9 KJV

A Learning Stage 83 – Cletus Returns

When you enter into a business arrangement with people you also have a personal relationship with it can often times make it difficult to enforce penalties. If both parties are not in complete compliance with all terms, it can put a strain on relationships and create a rift.

<u>Scenario</u>:

Paul: "But, Grams, if you get Cole to throw Cletus out he may kill him literally. Cole is a pro-boxer with a bad temper, and Cletus is a leech and an instigator. These are a bad combination and two explosive ingredients. Those two never got along. Cole loves you to death and would want to hurt anyone taking advantage of you, Grams. Don't tell Cole or get him involved."

Grandma: "What else can I do?"

Paul: "You have to get a good lawyer and evict Cletus."

Grandma: "Pay a lawyer to put out someone who isn't paying to be here in the first place? That's ridiculous. I watched that boy grow up, he better respect his elders and leave, or I'll give his stuff away."

Paul: "Please don't do that Grams, it's illegal. And Cletus is low enough to sue you for it."

Grandma: "Then I'll call the cops and have them put him out."

Paul: "They won't do it. It's a civil matter, not criminal."

Grandma: "You are mistaken on that, I'm sure of it. It's my house. He's my grandson, and I don't want him here anymore until he pays. My name is on the deed."

Paul: "Grams I'm telling you the police won't do anything their hands are tied. It's not a criminal offense it's civil."

She called the police who told her exactly what Paul said they would and informed her she had to go to court to get Cletus out. Not having gone to court before, she thought she would be given a one on one time with the judge who would call the police and tell them to kick Cletus out. Instead, she stood in several lines until she got the right one. The clerk said he could not give her legal advice and could only sell her the forms to complete to get a court date.

She returned home tired. She looked in the phone book and called an attorney and had an appointment to meet with him a few days later. He wanted to charge her just to talk to him and then to fill out paperwork. He told her it might take up to six months to get a court date to get Cletus out. She did not like that answer. She paid for the consult and left.

Discussion Questions:

1. Should Paul's grandmother allow Cole to settle this

matter and not bother the court?
2. Explain all the possible reasons why the police refused to intervene in this situation.
3. How would you advise this grandmother to resolve this matter?

Follow-up Suggestions:

- Unless absolutely necessary avoid doing business with friends and family
- Clearly outline your arrangements in writing
- Follow through with your written agreement and do not waiver. It is business!

Just for Fun:

Plaintiff's Attorney: What doctor treated you for the injuries you sustained while at work?
Plaintiff: Dr. Johnson.
Plaintiff's Attorney: And what kind of physician is Dr. Johnson?
Plaintiff: Well, I'm not sure, but I do remember that you said he was a good plaintiff's doctor.

*   *   *

The Court: Is there any reason why you couldn't serve as a juror in this case?
Potential Juror: I don't want to be away from my job that long.
The Court: Can't they do without you at work?
Potential Juror: Yes, but I don't want them to know that.

*   *   *

Defendant: Judge, I want you to appoint me another lawyer.
The Court: And why is that?

Defendant: Because the Public Defender isn't interested in my case.

The Court (addressing the public defender): Do you have any comments on the defendant's motion?

Public Defender: I'm sorry, Your Honor. I wasn't listening.

*   *   *

Wisdom is the principal thing; therefore get wisdom: and with all thy getting get understanding.
Proverbs 4:7 KJV
Withdraw thy foot from thy neighbour's house; lest he be weary of thee, and so hate thee
Proverbs 25:17 KJV

A Learning Stage 84 – Judge Leslie

Your best evidence is tangible corresponding documentation to dispute the tenants' arguments.

<u>Scenario</u>:

Landlord: "This is an easy case Judge Leslie. Hmm, Leslie for a guy judge?"

Judge: "Just refer to me as Judge."

Landlord: "Okay Judge Leslie. Anyway, the tenant was supposed to be out and when we got possession back it was a wreck."

Judge: "Pass the pictures up."

Landlord: "Look at him over there smiling like a Cheshire cat, the crook!"

Judge: "Don't talk to the defendant, talk to me."

Landlord: "Okay, Judge Leslie." < The landlord looked at the defendant > "You crook!"

Judge: "Pardon me?"

Landlord: "Sorry, I'm just so upset."

Tenant: "Your honor, I object to their whole case. I was never shown any pictures, video, receipts of any kind. I left the place in perfect condition and was not given a security itemization within the required

21 days. I want my full deposit returned and punitive damages because it's been 5 months."

Landlord: "What? Are you kidding me? The nerve after all the damage you caused? You crook!"

Judge: "Enough with the name calling. I told you, don't talk to him."

Landlord: "Okay Judge Leslie, but look at him over there smiling."

Judge: "I told you, just call me Judge or Judge Miller will do. Let's address the itemization, did you send him one within 21 days?"

Landlord: "Judge Leslie, there was a lot of damage. All the workers we called referred to it as a big job. They refused to write it up unless we guaranteed them the job. But I can tell you it would have cost 2-3 times his deposit. We knew that much."

Judge: "Is that a yes or no?"

Landlord: "We had to call Russell, who has done work for us before. He was on vacation and when he returned he had a real big job already lined up. Otherwise, he could've done it for us."

Judge: "Please just answer my question. Did you send him an itemization of his deposit?"

Landlord: "Yes."

Judge: "Within the 21 days of his move out?"

Landlord: "Yes."

Tenant: "They're lying. No they did not."

Judge: "Fine, that's in dispute. Pass up the itemization you sent to him, and tell me how you gave it to him?"

Landlord: "Here, this explains it all."

Judge: "There's a problem. Is this the only itemization you sent him?"

Landlord: "Yes."

Judge: "How did you get it to him?"

Landlord: "By mail."

Judge: "Where did you mail it? It has no address on it."

Landlord: "That's because he didn't give us a forwarding address."

Judge: "Then you mail it to the last address you had for him. I see another problem. You say you gave this one and only itemization to him within the twenty-one days?"

Landlord: "That's right."

Judge: "And there are no other itemizations or bills, just this one from Wreckhim Construction?"

Landlord: "That's right."

Judge: "The twenty one days ended March 21st and this bill was prepared May 1st. It indicates work began April 16 and was finished April 20th."

Landlord: "That's right. There the crook goes smiling again, Judge Leslie. Would you tell him to stop it! That proves just what I've been saying. I told you it was a lot of work, Judge Leslie. It took a whole crew of guys two weeks to do the job."

Tenant: "See, Your Honor, they just proved *my* case for me. They never sent me an itemization. I heard they had to do that in 21 days. I also heard through the grapevine they wanted to sue me because they thought they couldn't rent it. I asked for the itemization and the next day they hired Wreckhim. Then in May they filed this lawsuit against me. I moved out in February. This is now July."

Discussion Questions:

1. Did the landlord waive his rights to collect the security deposit? Explain.
2. Could the landlord lose the ability to recover the construction bill and end up paying the tenant full reimbursement of the deposit and 2 times the deposit in punitive? Explain.
3. Do you think the tenant left the property in good condition like he claimed? Explain.
4. Was the judge right to focus on the SDI deadline and documents so much? Explain.
5. How do you think the judge will rule? Why?
6. Do you agree with how you believe the judge will rule? Explain.

Follow-up Suggestions:

- Don't upset the judge
- Be respectful to everyone and to the judge's instructions

Just for Fun:

Several women appeared in court, each accusing the others of causing the trouble that they were having in the apartment building where they all lived.

The judge, with Solomon-like wisdom decreed, "Okay, I'm ready to hear the evidence...I'll hear from the oldest woman first."

The case was dismissed for lack of testimony.

*   *   *

Two small county judges both got arrested for speeding on the same day. Rather than call the state Supreme Court for a visiting judge, each agreed to hear the other's case.

The first judge took the bench while the second stood at the defendant's table, and admitted his guilt. The sentencing judge immediately suspended both the fine and costs.

They switched places. The second judge admitted that he was speeding, too. Thereupon the first judge immediately fined him $250 and ordered him to pay court costs.

The second judge was furious. "I suspended your fine and costs, but you threw the book at me!" he fumed. The first judge looked at him and replied, "This is the second such case we've had in here today. Someone has to get tough about all this speeding!"

*   *   *

Speak not evil one of another, brethren. He that speaketh evil of his brother, and judgeth his brother, speaketh evil of the law, and judgeth the law: but if thou judge the law, thou art not a doer of the law, but a judge.
James 4:11 KJV
If any man among you seem to be religious, and bridleth not his tongue, but deceiveth his own heart, this man's religion is vain.
James 1:26 KJV

A Learning Stage 85 – Hands On Disaster

A wise landlord must develop a knack for discernment.

Scenario:

Nora telephoned her friend, Gertie, to provide an update on Gertie's new tenants and rental property.

Nora: "I'm telling you, Gertie, these are not the type of people we want in this neighborhood. I've been watching them. They have a van you know. They're always bringing it to the house filled with boxes of brand new unopened items. That merchandise has to be stolen. You need to get rid of those people."

Gertie: "Thanks for telling me Nora. Boris and I will look into it."

Boris: "I see the look on your face Gertie and I don't want to hear it. I know you just finished talking to nosey Nora, and I'm busy enjoying reading the sports page. I have no desire to hear her gossip and you should pay no attention to it as well."

Gertie: "But she says they're storing stolen property in our rental."

Boris: "Sounds like a matter for the police to look into."

Gertie: "We have no proof."

Boris: "Even more reason to butt out. They pay their rent on time, they cause us no trouble. The only one complaining is nosey, Nora, whose perspective is warped at best. Gertie, leave this alone and stop listening to nosey, Nora."

Gertie telephoned Nora and enlisted her aid, which needed little prompting. She reminded Nora about the garage door key being hidden on the property. Nora used that information to gain entry to the garage where she took pictures of several boxes of brand new products unopened in their original boxes. As she was about to leave she thought having one of the items with its serial number would be good evidence. As she believed it was stolen property she was certain the tenants would not report it missing.

Nora completed approximately six of these covert operations on behalf of Gertie. Nora's family all knew what she was doing and her husband and children felt justified in opening and taking ownership of the merchandise. She later called Gertie to update her.

Nora: "I think the police are on to these people and probably close to moving in on them. Remember our neighbor, Theodore? He lives across the street from me. Theodore told me he's seen the police going to your property on several occasions and they told him they were investigating a string of thefts and that he should keep his eyes opened. So you tell me, why have we started having so many thefts only after these people moved in? So I called the police and they confirm the items reported stolen are the very items I've taken pictures of being in these people's garage. I think we have enough evidence now to nail them. If you go in there yourself and see the stolen goods, call the cops and let them in too, they can finally arrest them and put them away."

Gertie took Nora's advice and entered the property using her duplicate keys. She searched the inside of the house, then went into the garage. She was startled by the tenants who came home and surprised her. An argument ensued as both were accusing the other of being a thief and a criminal. The argument escalated into a physical fight. A neighbor called the police. Gertie was transported and treated for her injuries at the local hospital.

The tenants explained to the police they had been the victims of a series of small thefts of merchandise from their internet import/export business. They say they began to suspect the landlord as the thefts kept occurring and there were never any signs of forced entry.

Tenant: "Naturally, after feeling violated and unsafe for months, I came home and caught her in the act. She had no right to be inside our residence unannounced and was only here to steal more merchandise. When she refused to leave, we protected ourselves and tried to throw her out and she assaulted us. In self-defense we fought back and she got the losing end of the fight. Weren't we within our rights to defend ourselves?"

A LEARNING STAGE 3

<u>Discussion Questions</u>:

1. Was it wise to solicit Nora's assistance in this matter? Explain.
2. Whose advice should Gertie have adhered to? Explain.
3. Who was the thief in the string of burglaries in the neighborhood?
4. Why was it true the thefts did not begin until after the tenants moved into the neighborhood?
5. Does this qualify as self-defense?
6. Based on the evidence presented to the police, will Gertie be treated as an injured victim or a suspect?
7. Was Gertie lawfully in the property?
8. How should each party involved have handled this differently to avoid the horrible outcome that resulted?

<u>Suggestions</u>:

- Avoid vigilante behavior that could lead to criminal prosecution against you
- Do not commit illegal acts even if you have good intentions for doing so
- Always take necessary safety precautions and operate with company safeguards in place (do not go alone, let others know where you will be, etc.) and do not put yourself in harm's way unnecessarily
- Refrain from eliciting the aid of people you do not want to be responsible for as your agents
- Let the appropriate authorities handle situations you are not qualified to. If you suspect criminal activity, notify the police to look into it

Just for Fun:

Lawyer's creed:
- A man is innocent until proven broke.

*   *   *

A lawyer was walking down the street and saw an auto accident. He rushed over, started handing out business cards, and said, "I saw the whole thing. I'll take either side."

*   *   *

Attorney: Officer, what led you to believe the defendant was under the influence?
Witness: Because he was *argumentary* and couldn't *pronunciate* his words.

*   *   *

A wrathful man stirreth up strife: but he that is slow to anger appeaseth strife.
Proverbs 15:18 KJV
A froward man soweth strife: and a whisperer separateth chief friends.
Proverbs 16:28 KJV
He that is of a proud heart stirreth up strife: but he that putteth his trust in the Lord shall be made fat.
Proverbs 28:25 KJV
When the righteous are in authority, the people rejoice: but when the wicked beareth rule, the people mourn.
Proverbs 29:2 KJV
But if he will not hear thee, then take with thee one or two more, that in the mouth of two or three witnesses every word may be established.
Matthew 18:16 KJV
(23) Therefore if thou bring thy gift to the altar, and there rememberest that thy brother hath ought against thee;

(24) Leave there thy gift before the altar, and go thy way; first be reconciled to thy brother, and then come and offer thy gift.

Matthew 5:23-24 KJV

(25) Agree with thine adversary quickly, whiles thou art in the way with him; lest at any time the adversary deliver thee to the judge, and the judge deliver thee to the officer, and thou be cast into prison.

(26) Verily I say unto thee, Thou shalt by no means come out thence, till thou hast paid the uttermost farthing.

Matthew 5:25-26 KJV

A Learning Stage 86 – Don't Alter My Security

The chances of knowing what all the latest scams are that *professional* tenants use is slim. The best safeguard you have as a rental property owner is to educate yourself regularly and to operate with strong ethical business practices.

Scenario:

Connor is a tenant who has developed a strategy to use against landlords that has served him well. Case # 1 is an example of the many cases Connor has won with his scheme. Case # 2 represents the only case Connor may potentially lose in court because the landlord routinely followed through with a pattern of good business principles.

~ Case # 1 ~

Connor: "Your Honor, I'm suing for my security deposit and additional expenses to upgrade the premises. The landlord also violated my rights to privacy and entered illegally and stole personal items."

Landlord1: "I did no such thing."

Judge: "Sir, did you or did you not enter the premises

after April first?"

Landlord1: "No, I did not."

Connor: "Yes he did. I have several witnesses with me here in court that saw him."

Landlord1: "Well, I may have gone in there to do a repair or two, I don't remember."

Judge: "So then it is possible that you indeed entered without notice or permission when the plaintiff was not home?"

Landlord1: "Judge, he was suing me for upgrades and I needed to see what he was talking about so I could defend myself. Besides, I'm allowed to enter without notice if I deem it necessary."

Judge: "There must be an emergency. Was there an emergency?"

Landlord1: "Yes, he was suing me for upgrades and the case was in a few days. All that stuff he's claiming was in the property was never there. I didn't see a big screen TV, jewelry and all that other stuff he's claiming. Besides who would leave expensive stuff like that out in the open?"

Judges: "So, are you now admitting you did enter without giving notice?"

Landlord1: "Judge he's the one who gave me notice he was suing me. I had to be able to defend   myself, right?"

~ Case # 2 ~

Connor: "Your Honor, I'm suing for my security deposit and additional expenses to upgrade the premises. The landlord also violated my rights to privacy and entered illegally and stole personal items." < *He looked at the landlord* > "Do you have anything to say?"

Judge: "Don't talk to the defendant, talk to me."

Connor: "Yes, sir. Uhm, so anyway, I want to be reimbursed for my stolen items and also because we were not sent a security deposit itemization (SDI)."

Judge: "What would you like to say in your defense?"

Landlord2: "I see two issues here. It is whether or not we illegally entered the premises and removed the tenant's personal property, and whether we sent him an itemization form and credited him for alleged upgrades."

Connor: "Those upgrades are not alleged. I made them and should be paid for them."

Landlord2: "In answer to that your honor; I'd like to refer to page 3, paragraph 6 of the signed month-to-month rental agreement. It clearly states there is to be no alterations to the premises without written consent. So he is admitting he violated and breached our contract as we never gave permission to make structural changes to the premises."

Connor: "Okay, Judge, I see that here now, but I didn't know that. Besides, it's too late now, the improvement was made so shouldn't he have to pay for that?"

Judge: "You're responsible for the terms of the contract you signed."

Landlord2: "Now, regarding the Security Deposit Itemization (SDI), any discussion of that is premature. The plaintiff is still residing in the premises and has not vacated."

Judge: "Are you still residing at the property?"

Connor: "No. I moved out, I don't live there anymore."

Landlord2: "Your Honor, the plaintiff has made no official notification to us that he has indeed moved out. When we read the issues of this case, we immediately sent a certified letter asking   whether he intended to move out and the letter was returned after three attempts. So discussion of a security deposit makes no sense when the tenant is still residing in the property. As he still lives there, has the keys and has property there, we have and had no reason to enter."

Judge: "When did you move out?"

Tenant: "September first."

Landlord2: "Your Honor, his complaint says we allegedly took his property on September third. Not only that, we follow procedures to avoid such claims. We had no reason to enter the premises and have not been inside so we can't speak about its condition today. However, if he is giving me possession now, turning keys over to me in front of this court and attesting he's completely moved out and removed all his possessions, I will gladly enter and do my required SDI. I'll bear in mind his admitted breach in making unauthorized alterations and ask the court do the same. So that we're clear, am I to understand that's what he wants to do today to make this court appearance beneficial? Also, this allows us to inspect the premises so the security deposit issue can be resolved. The tenant is saying he has moved out as of today and will hand over the keys right now, thus relinquishing possession. If not, I believe we have nothing to discuss. He's still in possession and discussion of the security deposit is premature until after he vacates."

Judge: "Well, Mister Connor, would you like to turn possession over now?"

Connor: "Uh, I wasn't prepared to do that today. But if he's willing to pay me a few thousand dollars, I'll go ahead and give him the keys and move out."

Judge: "So you did lie to this court and in fact have *not* moved out."

Connor: "I didn't say that. I just, uh, can we continue the case on a later date?"

Discussion Questions:

1. Who do you think the judge will rule for and against in both cases?
2. Does Connor seem to be trying to pull a common scam on the landlords? Explain.
3. List the evidence or statements made in both cases that will help the prevailing party win.
4. Were both landlords prepared to defend themselves and present their side well?
5. If you had to be one of the two landlords, which would you prefer to be? Explain.

Follow-up Suggestions:

- Don't let tenants provoke you into fear and panic, do not march to their beat
- Operate by the law and do not act outside of that
- Do not resort to self-help
- Document your encounters and interactions with your tenants

- Much landlord/tenant conflict in court hinges on proof of the terms of the contract signed, the condition of the property at move-in and move-out, and the itemization of the security deposit

Just for Fun:

A small-town prosecutor called his first witness to the stand: a grandmotherly, elderly woman.

He approached her and asked, "Mrs. Jones, do you know me?"

She responded, "Why yes, I do know you, Mr. Williams. I've known you since you were a young boy. And frankly, you've been a big disappointment to me. You lie, you cheat on your wife, you manipulate people and talk about them behind their backs. You think you're a rising big shot when you haven't the brains to realize you will never amount to anything more than a two-bit paper pusher. Yes, I know you."

The lawyer was stunned. Not knowing what else to do, he pointed across the room and asked, "Mrs. Williams, do you know the defense attorney?"

She replied, "Why, yes I do. I've known Mr. Bradley since he was a youngster, too. I used to babysit him for his parents. And he, too, has been a real disappointment to me. He's lazy, racist, and he has a drinking problem. The man can't build a normal relationship with anyone, and his law practice is one of the shoddiest in the entire state. Yes, I know him."

At this point, the judge rapped the courtroom to silence and called both counselors to the bench.

In a very quiet voice, he threatened, "If either of you asks her if she knows me, you'll be jailed for contempt!"

*   *   *

He taketh the wise in their own craftiness: and the counsel of the froward is carried headlong.
Job 5:13 KJV
The way of a fool [is] right in his own eyes: but he that hearkeneth unto counsel [is] wise.
Proverbs 12:15 KJV
Hear counsel, and receive instruction, that thou mayest be wise in thy latter end.
Proverbs 19:20 KJV

A Learning Stage 87 – Crime Free Help

Call your local law enforcement agency for information on programs they have implemented to address your industry issues. Find out what your Crime Free Multi-Housing Program (CFMHP) offers as some provide benefits the others do not, from graffiti abatement to an assigned officer showing up in court on your behalf with "calls for service" data and other pertinent records; to demonstrate to the court your tenants are the source of criminal activity and police responses that create a nuisance.

Scenario:

Josie: "I'm not attending any Crime Free workshops this year or ever."
Darwin: "Why? You were learning so much."
Josie: "Yes, just enough to get me into trouble. Do you know how many times I could have been in trouble for acting on the information I learned? Several!"
Darwin: "Whose fault was that?"
Josie: "Not mine. I was only doing what the police told me to. They showed us what gang tattoos looked like, and for the first time I could distinguish between

an average tattoo and a gang or prison affiliated tattoo. But it only got me into trouble."

Darwin: "Whose fault was that?"

Josie: "Not mine. All I did was point out to people not to even bother filling out an application because I recognized they had gang tattoos and we didn't take criminals."

Darwin: "The police did not tell you to do that. That is why you need to take their information coupled with the information from Fair Housing to create a set of policies that abide by the law."

Josie: "It wasn't my fault. The way I see it, it's pointless to give me information I can't do anything with."

Darwin: "It sure would have helped that woman who rented her apartments to rival gang members and couldn't figure out why she had so many shootings. Remember how her complex was quickly bombarded with so many serious crimes that her good tenants moved out immediately. Her building was completely destroyed in such a short period of time and to this day she can't get it rented."

Josie: "And then there were those tenants that were doing drugs and now I could prove it because they showed us what the paraphernalia looked like."

Darwin: "Right, again not their fault. They didn't tell you to go over there and announce you were going to report them to the narcotics bureau of the police department. You could have made an informed call without putting yourself out there. You wanted them to know you were calling and hoped it would make them fearful of you and stop. Instead it backfired and they were aware you were giving information to the police about them and they retaliated."

Josie: "Well, what good is Crime Free? What advice should I take from them? What have they done for me? I don't think I want to be too closely involved with cops. We already have so many problems here with crimes, drugs, burglaries, you name it."

Darwin: "Did you invite the police for the inspection?"

Josie: "No way. I don't want them telling me what to do with my property to make some huge remodeling repairs that would cost more than what the building is worth."

Darwin: "Stop blowing things out of proportion. They are not code enforcement. The inspection is designed to give you some practical safety tips and things you can do to make your property less susceptible to being victimized and a haven for criminal activity."

Josie: "Well, you do it first, then come talk to me."

Darwin: "I did. Eight months ago. I went from four burglaries a month to none the last four months. The dealers stopped selling over here because they know the residents are watching, taking pictures of them and calling the police. I don't rent to people who will not sign the Crime Free Addendum. We actually took the training from that class to heart and found out how to work together with the police department to make our community safer and minimize our problems. Now the main people who come to ask about vacancies are people who are glad to sign and abide by the addendum. Once in a while we get someone fresh out of prison who comes but once they see our criteria and the addendum they don't come back. The way I see it, we all have to start somewhere and this program works if you participate and have good committed officers running it."

Josie: "Hmm, maybe I will go again and give this program another shot. It couldn't hurt."

Darwin: "Good for you. That's the right attitude. There's also no cost, just your time and   attention.   But that's the least we can pay to receive all the benefits."

Discussion Questions:

1. Was the Crime Free Program causing the crime in Josie's complex?
2. Was Josie doing her part to improve the conditions of her community?
3. List the benefits of a Crime Free Multi-Housing Program
4. Can these programs guarantee everyone will be satisfied and never have another crime or bad tenant on their property again? Explain
5. Were Josie's expectations reasonable?

Follow-up Suggestions:

Join a well-organized Crime Free Multi-Housing Program in your area that provides:

- Tips to recognize and deter criminal activity
- Practical advice to protect your property and not invite criminal elements
- The best locations to put security cameras

- Fair Housing laws
- Legal strategies from a qualified and competent landlord/tenant attorney
- Apartment Association advisor who shares the most common complaints received
- Resources of people and organizations to call for future assistance

<u>Just for Fun:</u>

A defendant in a lawsuit involving large sums of money was saying to his lawyer, "If I lose this case, I'll be ruined."

"It's in the judge's hands now," said the lawyer.

"Would it help if I sent the judge a box of cigars?" asked the defendant.

"Oh no!" said the lawyer. "This judge is a stickler for ethical behavior. A stunt like that would prejudice him against you. He might even find you in contempt of the court. In fact, you shouldn't even smile at the judge."

Within the course of time, the judge rendered a decision in favor of the defendant. As the defendant left the courthouse, he said to his lawyer, "Thanks for the tip about the cigars. It worked."

"I'm sure we would have lost the case if you'd sent them," said the lawyer.

"But I did send them," said the defendant.

"What?? You did?"

"Yes, That's how we won the case."

"I don't understand," said the lawyer.

"It's easy. I sent the cheapest cigars that I could find to the judge, but enclosed the plaintiff's business card."

*   *   *

Thy princes [are] rebellious, and companions of thieves: every one loveth gifts, and followeth after rewards: they judge not the fatherless, neither doth the cause of the widow come unto them.

Isaiah 1:23 KJV

And I will restore thy judges as at the first, and thy counsellors as at the beginning: afterward thou shalt be called, The city of righteousness, the faithful city.

Isaiah 1:26 KJV

Cease ye from man, whose breath [is] in his nostrils: for wherein is he to be accounted of?

Isaiah 2:22 KJV

Don't put your trust in mere humans. They are as frail as breath. What good are they?

Isaiah 2:22 NLT

Tell the godly that all will be well for them. They will enjoy the rich reward they have earned!

Isaiah 3:10 KJV

But the wicked are doomed, for they will get exactly what they deserve.

Isaiah 3:11 KJV

He that walketh with wise [men] shall be wise: but a companion of fools shall be destroyed.

Proverbs 13:20 KJV

A Learning Stage 88 – Plan to Change

There are admittedly many contradictions and issues with housing laws and how they are enforced. Complaints from a lone voice often get no action. If the real estate community learned to come together as a united group it would speak volumes toward being recognized as a powerful unit that could not be ignored.

Scenario:

Stan called his friend Corey to express his gratitude for the influence Stan had over Corey's son.

Stan: "Hey, thank you for that advertising quiz you sent my son. It scared him so much he no longer wants to get into this business. Ha-ha, that was a great joke. He had my granddaughter take it and she enrolled in classes and is attending a Fair Housing Workshop next month."

Corey: "I'm glad to hear your granddaughter took it as an opportunity to say to herself, 'I still want to do this. So I have to get information so I can do it right and not make these unavoidable mistakes.' That's good news. Now for the bad news. That quiz I sent you was not a joke. Those were actual documented words and phrases given as examples by Fair Housing that they consider as discriminatory language that convey a preference or limitation."

Stan: "What? I have used some of those terminologies and I wasn't trying to discriminate against anyone."

Corey: "If you want to continue using them and you're never challenged, no problem. But if you keep using them chances are eventually you will get called out on it and you will then have your chance to defend its use. I, personally, would prefer to avoid the whole problem. I don't have thousands of dollars to hire legal counsel to fight a war that is not that important to me. I look at it this way. These are common phrases that for some reason many have found offensive. Since I'm sensitive to that and it is defeating my purpose, I just choose not to use them."

Stan: "That's a bit cowardice don't you think?"

Corey: "You might be right about that. So tell me what your proactive plan is to fight this issue since you feel so strongly about it?"

Stan: "Huh? Plan?"

Corey: "Right. My plan isn't good enough for you, it is cowardice by your assessment. Evidently you have a better way, so I'm patiently waiting to hear yours."

Stan: "Uh, well, I just think you could..."

Corey: "I'm going to stop you there, because I'm a coward remember. So let's leave me out of it. You are the brave one in this, so if you want me to hear your criticism, it falls on deaf ears unless you start with what *you* plan to do. Tell me about your pro-active plan that is so much better than mine."

Stan: "Uh, well, I don't have one."

Corey: "Then you haven't earned the right to criticize mine."

Stan: "What is your plan I haven't heard it?"

Corey: "You've experienced it. My plan is to create awareness and share the things I learn with others in the business and help them avoid unnecessary liabilities. My plan is not to be critical of an enforcing agent unless I have a better way and am actively doing something to change or improve. I don't want to get people stirred up and feel even more justified doing things wrong or disgruntled about complying with the law. That will not help them. I want to inspire them to want to know more, protect themselves, get informed, and if so inspired to rally a team of people committed to make positive changes."

Stan: "I would say I am sorry if I didn't have my foot in my mouth. I apologize."

Discussion Questions:

1. When you discover a good piece of information do you share it?
2. Do you have a plan of being proactive and a help to others in this profession?
3. How often do you complain about the injustices you have experienced?
4. According to Corey, are you someone who has earned the right to complain?
5. Are you learning new things each month? You should!

Just for Fun:

My son was fired from his job at the road department for stealing. I have to say I saw it coming. The last time I was at his house all the signs were there.

*   *   *

But avoid foolish questions, and genealogies, and contentions, and strivings about the law; for they are unprofitable and vain.

Titus 3:9 KJV

A Learning Stage 89 – Discriminate Offenses

The housing laws have a way of fluctuating quite often. Those enforcing these statutes can place their own interpretation on the ordinances at the unfortunate detriment to rental property owners. Currently there is much confusion about recent changes on the alleged discriminatory merits of rejecting applicants with criminal backgrounds.

<u>Scenario</u>:

Boss: "Henry, you know why I've asked you into my office right?"

Henry: "Yes. I brought all my notes for the people I've screened within the last 6 months. I cannot imagine why someone would say I treated them unfairly."

Boss: "Do you remember Mister Capricio and Mister Hall? Let's start with them."

Henry: "No, the names don't ring a bell."

Boss: "Mister Capricio was denied tenancy because he had a conviction of statutory rape on his record."

Henry: "Yes Ma'am, that's correct. He is a registered sex offender. I didn't know why, but he admitted he had to register."

Boss: "Would it change your decision to know the offense was committed over 20 years ago? It's his one and only conviction. He was underage himself at the time. He lived in another state and fathered a child. The parents of the girl were so angry when they found out they called the police and pressed charges. When they reached legal age they got married and have had 3 more children. They are still married today."

Henry: "Yes, that information would have changed my decision to reject him."

Boss: "I see. What about Mister Hall? You accepted him and he is a registered sex offender as well."

Henry: "Yes, but although he still has to register as a sex offender, he shared the details of his case with me. He said he could show me documented proof that his conviction was overturned. But unfortunately, the system doesn't think it important to straighten out not forcing him to continue registering. I couldn't deliver another poor injustice to the guy and deny him after all he's been through."

Boss: "I see. What about Mrs. Jefferson. You accepted her and she has a *recent* conviction of being a sex offender."

Henry: "Okay, boss, prepare to be amazingly proud. She was a high school teacher and the kid she was with would have turned 18 a few months after the incidents. Not only does something like that give a boy mega bragging rights, but, I covered myself and attached a picture of her driver's license. Let me tell you, boss, that's not offensive."

Boss: "I noticed that, and I wondered why you photocopied her license prematurely."

Henry: "Now you understand, right? Have you got a look at her? Wow!"

Boss: "I see. Now to Mister Cohen, he was also accepted by you."

Henry: "Okay, boss, I know he had felony drug convictions. But it occurred a long time ago and he told me he entered a program where he met and married his wife. He's become a family man and has not been arrested since then."

Boss: "I see. You made a lot of decisions based on what these applicants did and did not tell you."

Henry: "What makes you say that?"

Boss: "Two things. One, what you have told me. Two, because they were all *testers* sent from a friend of mine to do me a favor."

Henry: "No kidding. I passed with flying colors, right?"

Discussion Questions:

1. Do you believe the boss is happy with all four of Henry's decisions? Explain.
2. Did Henry discriminate against any of the testers? Explain.
3. Had the testers been from Fair Housing, would Henry have been in violation of any housing laws? Explain.

Follow-up Suggestions:

- Provide ongoing training to your staff to help them understand the law
- Quiz your staff to be certain they both use and know your written criteria

Just for Fun:

One Liner Performance Evaluations...
- He has a full 6-pack, but lacks the plastic thingy to hold it all together.
- He has reached rock bottom and has started to dig.
- He donated his brain to science before he was done using it.
- If brains were taxed, she would get a large refund.
- Some drink from the fountain of knowledge, he only gargles.
- She needs more to do. Might I be so bold as to suggest looking for another job?
- The gates are down, lights are flashing, but the train just is not coming.
- She is a clock watcher who is in a different time zone than the rest of us.
- This employee should go far — and the sooner he starts, the better.
- This young man has delusions of adequacy.

*　　　*　　　*

A murder trial was underway in Philadelphia. Although there was strong circumstantial evidence against the defendant, the victim's body was never discovered.

In desperation, the defense attorney took a gamble and got creative with his closing statement. He said, "Ladies and gentlemen of the jury, I have a surprise for all of you." He looked down at his wristwatch and continued, "In sixty seconds, the alleged victim in this case, who is presumed dead will walk into this courtroom."

He and the jurors focused their attention on the courtroom door. Two minutes passed. Nothing happened.

The defense lawyer challenged the jury members' integrity. He said, "I will admit I made up my previous statement. But you must confess that you all looked at that door with anticipation. I, therefore, contend there is indeed reasonable doubt in this case as to whether the victim was killed. No one can attest to the well-being of the alleged victim and without evidence of a crime, I insist that you return a verdict of not guilty."

The confused and bewildered jury left the room to deliberate. Within minutes the jury returned and announced a guilty verdict.

"What! How?" defense counsel inquired. "I saw each and every one of you stare at that door. So I know there was doubt."

The jury foreman replied, "You are right, all the members of the jury did look. But your client didn't."

*   *   *

Likewise, ye younger, submit yourselves unto the elder. Yea, all [of you] be subject one to another, and be clothed with humility: for God resisteth the proud, and giveth grace to the humble.
1 Peter 5:5 KJV
Nevertheless, whereto we have already attained, let us walk by the same rule, let us mind the same thing.
Philippians 3:16 KJV

A Learning Stage 90 – Disability Dilemma

Handling situations that involve a protected class can be uncomfortable and cause a landlord to second guess his judgment. Landlords may question everything they say or do. The more information they obtain the more uncertain and skeptical they become.

<u>Scenario</u>:

A man in a wheelchair with a blanket draped over his legs wheeled himself into a property management company. He caught the attention of the two managers as he almost purposely seemed to thrust the wheels of his wheelchair into the receptionist's desk. He was seen handing the receptionist his completed application and then being directed to Manager1's desk. Manager2 was more experienced so she kept a watchful eye on the processing of this applicant who was eventually informed he was accepted and welcomed to the apartment complex.

Applicant: "I would also like to request a closer parking space."
Manager1: "I'm sorry but I didn't see a doctor

authorization with your application and..."

Manager2: "Psst! Let me speak with you in private for a moment."

Manager2 found it necessary to interject and call Manager1 away to the back of the room. The two managers had a private conversation. Manager2 reprimanded Manager1, "This man has an obvious disability. The law says in cases like these a doctor authorization is not necessary."

Manager1 accepted the applicant as a tenant and switched the parking space for his apartment with one that was much closer.

Three months later, the tenant was seen walking around the complex by several people. Management sent the tenant a letter that indicated, "Effective immediately you have been reassigned parking space #62 because you no longer qualify for space #2. If you dispute this finding and modification because you believe you do still qualify to retain the accommodation afforded you, please provide a doctor's written authorization that complies with our written policy regarding modifications and accommodations. We have attached our policy and form regarding this issue should you have any questions."

The tenant called his local housing agency to place a complaint against the management company. He claimed he had been discriminated against and management had threatened to take away his close parking spot so they could replace it with one far away simply because they did not like him.

Upon looking into the situation and hearing from management the housing agent was able to conclude the complaint was unfounded. The tenant had broken both of his legs in a skiing accident, and both legs were still in a cast when he was accepted as a tenant. His legs healed and the casts were removed. He made a conscious choice not to tell management his disability was temporary because he wanted to keep the close parking space. He was prepared to challenge any illegal inquiries about the nature of his disability and had familiarized himself with the law before applying.

The tenant's attempt to mislead management was not looked at favorably. The manager's due diligence to try to comply with the law was helpful. They also had good documentation and rather than assume or accuse the tenant of being less than forthcoming, gave him a chance to keep the accommodation provided he complied with their written policy.

Discussion Questions:

1. Was manager1 right to ask for a doctor's note when the new tenant asked for a closer parking space?
2. Was manager2 wrong to override manager1's request for a doctor's note?
3. Should everyone requesting a disabled variance be required to provide proof of the disability regardless if it appears obvious or not?
4. Would these managers be justified in being more strict and probing toward any applicant claiming to have a disability to insure they are not fooled again?
5. Is there anything wrong with a landlord or manager

asking as many question as necessary until becoming comfortable that an applicant is indeed disabled and in need of an accommodation or modification?

Follow-up Suggestions:

- Err on the side of caution, comply with the law
- Do not put added pressure on yourself to make a medical determination about one's disability
- If it appears by all legal standards that one qualifies for a variance then provide it
- Should you have compelling evidence you were lied to and discover the tenant is taking advantage of an accommodation that rightfully should be extended to one truly in need of it, do not rush to judgment
- It is best to have a written policy to follow in these matters

Just for Fun:

There are two men walking on the street. One approaches the other and asks, "Have you seen a cop?"
"No," the other man answers.
"Good," the first man replies, "stick 'em up!"

*   *   *

My son, keep my words, and lay up my commandments with thee.
Proverbs 7:1 KJV
We all make many mistakes, but those who control their tongues can also control themselves in every other way.
James 3:2 NLT

So also, the tongue is a small thing, but what enormous damage it can do. A tiny spark can set a great forest on fire.

James 3:5 NLT

Who is a wise man and endued with knowledge among you? let him show out of good conversation his works with meekness of wisdom.

James 3:13 KJV

But the wisdom that is from above is first pure, then peaceable, gentle, and easy to be entreated, full of mercy and good fruits, without partiality, and without hypocrisy.

James 3:17 KJV

And those who are peacemakers will plant seeds of peace and reap a harvest of goodness.

James 3:18 NLT

A Learning Stage 91 – Court Recovery?

There are times when taking court action is necessary to resolve your dispute. Be certain you are being reasonable filing your lawsuit or the court may not look favorably on your case.

<u>Scenario</u>:

Judge: "Your tenants lived there for ten years and you're suing for the maximum of $7,500? They paid their rent on time each month during their tenancy. You say you tried to handle this out of court but they were being unreasonable? Okay, explain how you arrived at the $7,500 and then I'll address the countersuit."

Landlord: "We had brand new carpeting, the appliances were fairly new, new paint job, we gave them our washer and dryer, and we told them they could have our old furniture. We not only lived in that home ourselves, we raised our children there. So we did a lot for these people. They give us two weeks' notice that they're moving out, as if they did us a favor. It's not our fault he lost his job. They owe us for the whole month and in California they have to give 60 days' written notice that they are going to move out when they have been there longer than one year."

Judge: "When did they tell you they intended to move? When did you confirm they moved out, and when did they actually move?"

Landlord: "On January 31st they said they would be moving out and felt they could be out by the fourteenth of February and gave me half of February's rent saying it was all they could afford. Then on the seventh of February they told me they were moved out and I met with them at the property and all their belongings were gone. They returned the key as well. It could have been cleaned better."

Judge: "So what was the condition of the property on the seventh of February?"

Landlord: "Like I said, maybe you weren't listening, it could have been cleaned better. The carpet is filthy, it couldn't be cleaned, it had to be replaced. This time I installed hardwood floors, and because my son and I did the work it cost only $6,500. It cost another $1,000 to paint, clean, replace 3 outlet covers and six screws. It's all written there in my complaint. I still don't know why that dumb attorney of mine I talked to about this, who wouldn't take the case, said I couldn't charge them for the washer and dryer, appliances and furniture."

Judge: "Perhaps because you gifted it to them."

Landlord: "So the least they could do is gift new products to the next guy and not be so selfish. We gave it to them as a nice gesture to a young couple starting out. I admit since we planned to buy new stuff for our new house it saved us the trouble of moving those items or figuring out what charity to give it to, but still."

Judge: "Then we can leave those items out because you are not out any money for the items you gifted to them."

Landlord: "I guess that's true. But it would cost me thousands more to replace them."

Judge: "Did your contract state they must replace those items upon move out?"

Landlord: "Well, no, but I figured they would know to do that. I mean it's common courtesy."

Judge: "Please pass up your paperwork."

~ Later ~

Judge: "I only see a bill for $200 that reads, 'cleaning up after construction.'"

Landlord: "Right, that's all I have."

Judge: "They say they cleared the place out and left it clean. You say it could have been cleaner. The property was cleaned on April 30th, April 30th? And it looks like they were cleaning up from the installation of the hardwood floors, and painting. Have you even looked at this receipt you handed me?"

Landlord: "What! Those dummies wrote that on the receipt?"

Judge: "Sir if you want to recover damages, you must prove it and have corresponding receipts to back it up.

Landlord: "But judge, we did most of the work. I wrote on

the complaint how much it cost for that. I didn't know I needed more than that. If you want me to write up a receipt, I can do it right now. Give me a moment, sounds like a lot of nonsense to me."

Judge: "Where's the Security Itemization? You look confused. Did you send them the reasons for the deductions along with receipts as you are claiming more than $125?"

Landlord: "I was too busy fixing the place up. I had them served with the complaint and it had the amounts of the deductions, so yes that itemized the security."

Tenant: "Your honor, we have a countersuit. We left the property clean, and even paid for extra days we did not live there. We never complained and the carpet needed to be replaced when we moved in. We tried to do the right thing, rather than mooching off the landlord after losing my job, we voluntarily left and moved in with family. We're sorry we couldn't have given more notice but we thought the sooner we got out the sooner he could get new tenants. He withheld our security deposit all this time and the first time we hear why was when we were served with papers he was suing us in June. We really need our money. I'm sorry things did not work out between us, but can he do what he did?"

Discussion Questions:

1. Was the landlord being reasonable? Explain.
2. Who do you believe the judge will rule in favor of? Explain.

3. Was the landlord wise to bring this lawsuit? Why or why not?
4. What should the landlord have done differently to avoid a court case?
5. Indicate all statements you believe hurt the landlord's case.

Follow-up Suggestions:

- Let documented facts do most of your talking for you
- Do your best to mitigate your damages and prevent a court from intervening
- If you must go to court, be prepared

Just for Fun:

Q: What's the difference between God and a lawyer?
A: God does not think he is a lawyer!

*   *   *

This is a faithful saying, and these things I will that thou affirm constantly, that they which have believed in God might be careful to maintain good works. These things are good and profitable unto men.

Titus 3:8 KJV

A Learning Stage 92 – Pet Dilemma

Your policies should be clearly understood and equally enforced. When you waive a rule for one tenant, other tenants feel justified in bending the rules.

Scenario:

Jody was outside her apartment with her older brother, feeding her new puppy treats. The only problem with this is the apartment complex Jody's family resided in is a "no pet" building. Sal, the manager was making his rounds and turned his head to look away.

The following week, Bruce, a problem tenant is seen walking a Saint Bernard into his apartment. Sal confronted Bruce, who admitted he had just acquired the dog as his pet.

Sal: "Listen, Bruce, you have lived here 6 months and you know this is a 'no-pet' building. Here's a 'Three-Day Notice' that if you don't get rid of the dog we will evict you."

Bruce: "Evict me for what?"

Sal: "Read the notice. It will explain it all in black and white."

Bruce: "No. I want you to explain it to me. Explain why everybody else can have a dog except me."

Sal: "Everybody else? No one else has a dog except you."

Bruce: "Liar!"

Sal: "Are you comparing yourself to little Jody? Look Bruce she just lost her father and I'm betting they got her that puppy to cheer her up. Besides that, she has a teeny little puppy that will grow to be a tiny little dog. You come strutting in with this monstrous sized beast to live in your itsy bitsy apartment."

Bruce: "My how things change. It was a spacious apartment when you were trying to sell me on moving in. Now it's miraculously shrunk. I think the rent should too."

Sal: "I'm done talking to you. If that *horse* is still here after three days, you're both out of here. I can't believe the nerve of some people like you, who'd attempt to compare themselves with the plight of an innocent young girl and her adorable puppy."

Discussion Questions:

1. Could this situation potentially be a Fair Housing violation? Explain.
2. Does a housing provider have the legal right to set a pet policy?
3. Can a housing provider make distinctions between the types and sizes of pets without violating Fair Housing laws?
4. If management had a written no pet policy, what if anything in the above scenario may have negated it? Explain.

5. Do you have a pet policy that addresses this issue?
6. What should management do now to straighten out this situation?

<u>Follow-up Suggestions</u>:

- Be consistent in your enforcement
- A delay in addressing breaches in your lease can later be seen as waivers
- Use your apartment association Pet Addendum as they annually update their forms
- Remember Pet Addendums do not apply to service or companion animals

<u>Just for Fun:</u>

Flash: Don't you have any lawyers here?

Judges: We solved our lawyer problem a long time ago. However, you could speak for him, if you wish. But be aware, if you lose, you'll share the same penalty as the accused.

Flash: The same penalty? You mean...that's crazy!

Judge: No, that's how we solved our lawyer problem.

*　　*　　*

The Court: "You may call your next witness."

Defendant's Attorney: "Your Honor, at this time I would like to swat opposing counsel on the head with his client's deposition."

The Court: "You mean read it?"

Defendant's Attorney: "No, Sir. I mean to swat him on the head with it. Pursuant to 'Rule 32,' I may use the deposition 'for any purpose' and that's the purpose I want to use it for."

The Court: "Well, it does say that."

    < Quiet pause. >

The Court: "There being no objection, you may proceed."

Defendant's Attorney: "Thank you, Judge."

    Thereafter, Defendant's attorney swatted plaintiff's attorney on the head with the deposition.

Plaintiff's Attorney (the victim): "But Judge ..."

The Court: "Next witness."

Plaintiff's Attorney: "... We object."

The Court: "Sustained. Next witness."

          *   *   *

But he that doeth wrong shall receive for the wrong which he hath done: and there is no respect of persons.
Colossians 3:25 KJV

A Learning Stage 93 – Surcharge

When a seemingly profitable business decision has been acceptable for decades, it can be difficult to understand the need for change.

<u>Scenario</u>:

Three vacancies were filled in January at an apartment complex. The Whites were composed of a mother, father, grandmother and two children. The Black family was made up of two sisters and their older brother. The Brown family was a single father and his daughter.

The apartments the three families chose to reside in have the same floor plan and are 4-bedroom apartments. The rent is $2000 a month. All three groups signed a one-year lease that indicated a surcharge of $150 would be due for each additional occupant accepted and added to the lease after signing.

Six months later Mr. Brown acquires full custody of his son and now wants to add him on the lease as an additional occupant. The Black's elderly aunt who was given less than six months to live wants to live her final days around her nieces and nephew. They want to accommodate her request and let her move in.

In September Mr. Brown wants to move his pregnant girlfriend in with them. The baby is due in November and they planned to have a wedding in October. He is upfront with all these details and asks to add his fiancé to his lease.

Discussion Questions:

1. List which, if any, of the three families' whose rent will change and to what amount.
2. Should any of the families be given a waiver to the surcharge? If yes, explain.
3. How can you justify the surcharge for the tenants you did not waive the fee for?
4. What arguments could the families give against the surcharges?
5. Do you see any legal issues with surcharges? Explain in detail.
6. Are surcharges a Fair Housing violation?

Follow-up Suggestions:

1. Charge a reasonable rent that will cover the expenses for your occupancy standards
2. If you have a lease, you are stuck with the amount of rent you agreed to. In a month to month agreement the rent amount can be modified with proper notice
3. When everyone is treated equally you can avoid such dilemmas
4. With a good contract, fair guidelines, and updated

training, this situation would be an easy decision. It is complicated however; if you are unaware it is an issue that raises interesting legalities

Just for Fun:

One Liners
- Good lawyers worry about facts, great lawyers worry about their opponents.
- A lawyer is someone who takes a lot of your money for helping you to take a little of someone else's money.
- Lawyers are not all liars. It's only the 98% of them who give the others a bad name.
- Salespeople are deal makers. Lawyers are deal breakers.
- Lawyers only lie when their lips move.

*   *   *

Thou shalt not wrest judgment; thou shalt not respect persons, neither take a gift: for a gift doth blind the eyes of the wise, and pervert the words of the righteous.

Deuteronomy 16:19 KJV

A Learning Stage 94 – Choosing Smart

The real estate industry requires the ability to make several judgment calls. Often these choices will not be popular and we may not fully understand the reasoning behind them.

<u>Scenario</u>:

Gil: "Hello, Mrs. Bighaut? This is, Gil, from Integrity Homes. I have good news for you. We just received a completed application from what looks like some good applicants."

Bighaut: "Oh really? Did you take a photograph of them this time like we asked?"

Gil: "No. I explained to you that we don't do that."

Bighaut: "Mercy! Can't you follow simple instructions, son? Now you said you couldn't do certain things so we told you we'd help you out with that. We make the final decision. If you take a photo of them and send it to us then we'll tell you yes or no."

Gil: "Yes, you clearly relayed that to me but…"

Bighaut: "So tell me what do these people look like?"

Gil: "They look like good applicants who…"

Bighaut: "You know that's not what I'm asking. Are they at least in this country legally?"

Gil: "They have good credit and a good rental history. There is no history of criminal..."

Bighaut: "Do they have children? We don't want children tearing our home up?"

Gil: "Mrs. Bighaut, I recommend you accept these people."

Bighaut: "No. You won't describe them, so I can tell they won't fit in with the neighborhood. You won't say whether they have kids so that tells me they do have a bunch of crumb snatcher. I don't like the people you choose and I told you unless you tell me what I want to know, I'll reject them. It's our properties and we say who lives there, not you!"

Gil: "You've made that very clear. However, we operate by the law and..."

Bighaut: "Mercy! Son, don't preach to me about the law. We refuse to harbor *illegals*, that's against the law. We will not house immorality and..."

Gil: "I'm well aware of your stance. I wish you could understand that my way gets everybody what they want. You get qualified tenants who pay their rent, and the renters receive a nice place to live. The neighborhood gets people who are hard workers who have shown to be good neighbors in the past. It's a win-win for everybody."

Bighaut: "Sure, son, sure. Easy for you to say. You don't have to live next door to these people. You just put them in our home and walk away."

Gil: "No, ma'am, I'm in this with you too. I have to deal with them and I try not to put in problem tenants."

Bighaut: "Nice speech, son. The answer is still, no!"

A LEARNING STAGE 3

<u>Discussion Questions</u>:

1. What should Gil do now?
2. The property does belong to the Bighauts, so should Gil follow their requests?
3. Can Gil override the owners' decision and accept the applicants?
4. What should the Bighauts do? Why?
5. If Integrity Homes violates Fair Housing rules because their client refused to listen would they be absolved of any and all responsibility? Explain.
6. List any and all violations Mrs. Bighaut was encouraging Gil to commit.

<u>Follow-up Suggestions</u>:

- Do not encourage your managers to violate the law and put their license at risk
- Managers make the attempt to explain the law to your clients

<u>Just for Fun</u>:

One liners
- I started out with nothing and still have most of it left.
- I pretend to work. They pretend to pay me.
- Sarcasm is just one more service we offer.
- If I throw a stick, will you leave?
- If I want to hear the pitter patter of little feet in my rentals, I'll put shoes on my cats.
- Does your train of thought have a caboose?
- Errors have been made. Others will be blamed.
- Stupidity is not a handicap. Park elsewhere!

- My husband and I divorced over religious differences. He thought he was God and I did not.
- If you cannot be kind, at least have the decency to be vague.

*   *   *

You have heard me teach things that have been confirmed by many reliable witnesses. Now teach these truths to other trustworthy people who will be able to pass them on to others.

2 Timothy 2:2 NLT

But shun profane and vain babblings: for they will increase unto more ungodliness.

2 Timothy 2:16 KJV

But foolish and unlearned questions avoid, knowing that they do gender strifes.

2 Timothy 2:23 KJV

And the servant of the Lord must not strive; but be gentle unto all [men], apt to teach, patient,

2 Timothy 2:24 KJV

A Learning Stage 95 – Critic Cal

<u>Scenario</u>:

A seventeen-year-old was observing his parents at work. They owned and operated a property management company. He attended seminars with his parents, as they hoped he would fall in their footsteps and enter the business.

He watched as his mother fielded calls from prospective tenants back to back. "Mom, how do you keep track of all those calls? You must have a good memory because I did not see you write any notes down."

Mother: "Who has time? You saw how many calls I got. I suppose I should use that form we created but I lost track of it. I created a filing system for your father and he was supposed to file it away."

He then focused his attention on his father, Cal, and observed him going through boxes of papers.

Son: "What are you doing, dad?"

Cal: "Trying to find some paperwork. We have some folks suing us, and our attorney wants us to provide him with some requested documents."

165

Son: "Mom said she created a filing system for you."

Cal: "Yes, she did. But who has time to keep up with such things?"

Son: "Why are they suing?"

Cal: "One says we made inappropriate inquiries about their protected class and then denied them tenancy. Another says we discriminated against them charging them more than others because of their protected class."

Son: "Mom says she created a form of questions to consistently ask everyone the same questions."

Cal: "Good thing she did too. Fortunately, she was using that form during the time the person called. We need that as evidence to show the questions we asked were appropriate and consistent."

Son: "Great! Once you find it, you can duplicate it and continue using it again. That way you can use it to defend yourself if it happens again."

Cal: "You're so young and idealistic. You have a lot to learn about the world. It's not that simple. Who has time to whip out a form and use it every time someone calls in? You've been at this how long? Oh that's right zero days."

Son: "Sorry, dad. I suppose you don't…How can I help?"

Cal: "Look in those file cabinets over there and see if you can find the rule thing we used to give out with the applications."

Son: "You mean the Application Procedure?"

Cal: "Yes, that's it. That thing and the sheet we created to decide who to take and reject."

Son: "You mean your Criteria?"

Cal: "Yes. We decided to change some things and we

need to find the dates of the changes."

Son: "I remember those two things coming up quite often at the training classes."

Cal: "How about less talking and more searching, son."

Cal's mother's neighbor walked into his office and produced a sealed envelope.

Neighbor: "Hey, Cal, your mother asked me to bring you this important note."

Cal: "Okay, thank you. Let me pay you for your time and gas to come here."

Neighbor: "It's not necessary. Your mother took care of that."

Son: "What is it, dad?"

Cal: "I don't know what I'm going to do with my mother. She will never learn, and is so stubborn she refuses to listen. Just because she's been on this earth longer she thinks she has all the answers. The note says she has a prescription ready to be picked up. So instead of calling she pays her neighbor to drive over here to deliver this note she wrote."

Son: "Wow. You bought her a computer and pay her internet service and I taught her how to use the email."

Cal: "She thinks it is too much money for the electricity to send emails. She is more comfortable with handwritten notes and the U.S. postal service. She thinks it's less money and trouble and I can't convince her otherwise. She says email is too much trouble, *who has the time*, she says."

Son: "Didn't you also buy her a cellular phone? I put all the numbers from her phone book into it and showed her how simple it is to use and to text."

Cal: "I know. She insists on having personal face to face interactions and thinks anything other than that is troublesome and time consuming. She doesn't see how learning to utilize a few modern conveniences can help her simplify her life and minimize costs and problems. Some people are so arrogant and stuck in their ways and they just won't listen to anyone younger than them, especially their own son who might possibly have some wisdom that could help them. No, they're much too proud to think someone with less life experience has anything of value to offer. I'm so glad I'm not like that!"

Discussion Questions:

1. Was Cal guilty of any of the things he was criticizing his mother for? Explain.
2. Are there highly recommended tasks you avoid doing because you find it tedious?
3. Have you and your staff learned to use social media to your advantage?
4. What are some things the younger generation could teach the older generation?
5. List some things an experienced manager could teach a new employee eager to learn?

Follow-up Suggestions:

- Embrace technological advances that help you conduct your business more efficiently
- The collaboration of each staff member's skills can

make a company strong
• Be open and willing to stretch your knowledge and abilities

Just for Fun:

An insurance agent called our medical office. One of our doctors had filled out a medically necessary leave-of-absence form for a patient, but, the agent said, the patient had altered it. The giveaway? The return-to-work date had been changed to February 30.

*   *   *

A 93 year old set of triplets found that living on their own was a struggle. They were the only and oldest living family members. They collectively and unanimously concluded it would be wise to move in together and they could help one another.

Two of the sisters were relaxing at home as the third was on her way back from a doctor's appointment.

Sister1: "How much do you want to bet she's badmouthing the two of us to everyone riding with her?"

Sister2: "That's not even worth betting, it's a given. As bad as her memory is, she has nerve to talk about us. Her memory is horrible. She would've forgotten to go to the doctor if we hadn't reminded her."

Sister1: "That is so true. I wonder how someone could be in such denial and not see their own flaws?"

Sister2: "I don't know either. If I were her, I'd not criticize others."

Sister1: "Right. Well, guess I'll go upstairs and take a bath."

TERESA BILLINGSLEY

~ 5 minutes later the third sister arrived home. ~

Sister3: "I'm back. Where is our sister?"
Sister2: "She just went upstairs to take a bath."
Sister3: "I hope she remembers to turn the water on and get in the tub this time."
Sister2: "Give her a break. I heard the water going so she remembered. Poor thing, her memory is really bad. I do hope she hasn't forgotten to take her clothes off."

Sister1 is heard calling down from upstairs, "Can I get some help up here. I got one foot   in the tub and I can't remember if I was about to take a bath or just finished one."

Sister2: "I better get up there and help the old woman. Tee hee, I'm so glad I'm not that bad."

Sister2 gets midway up the stairs and suddenly stopped to pause. She was heard calling out from the stairs, "Would someone please help me. I can't remember if I was going up the stairs or coming down."

Sister3 began laughing hysterically and said to herself aloud in criticism, "Those two are so pathetic. I certainly hope I don't become as bad as them. I'm so grateful I'm so much more coherent than the two of them. Knock on wood." Sister3 tapped her knuckles on the wooden coffee table in front of her, then replied. "Nobody move! I'll get the door it's probably my ride to drive me to my doctor's appointment."

*   *   *

There is one lawgiver, who is able to save and to destroy: who art thou that judgest another?

James 4:12 KJV

Therefore to him that knoweth to do good, and doeth it not, to him it is sin.

James 4:17 KJV

A Learning Stage 96 – Okay, Jose, Not!

Anyone who does work for you as a rental property owner and has interaction with prospective tenants should be trained and well versed in the housing laws for your jurisdiction.

Scenario:

Grady, and his son, Pablo, were hired to do some work on a rental property. The owner of the rental gave strict instruction to Grady that he expected would be adhered to.

"Ding dong"
~ The doorbell rings ~

Grady: "Yes? May I help you, Jose?"

Rudy: "Jose? Listen, I saw the 'for rent' sign in the front yard and I was wondering if…"

Grady: "Okay, Jose. Come on in and take a look around. We're still getting the place ready but I don't think they'd mind if you took a peek."

Pablo: <whispering to his father> "But, dad, the owners said not to let anyone in and to tell people to call them to see inside."

Grady: "Calm down, Jose. They didn't mean that."

~ Rudy walked around the house a few minutes ~

Rudy: "Excuse me but what caused that blood stain in that room in there?"

Grady: "Don't worry, Jose, my son and I will clean that out and you won't even know it was ever there. The cops are done investigating and collecting evidence. We've already cleaned up so..."

Rudy: "Police? Evidence? You know what? Listen I'm not interested any..."

Grady: "Calm down, Jose, they're not the immigration police. Besides, this area, well the whole neighborhood is really a good one. It's really a safe place to live. The guy that got murdered was an accident, or accidental...Son, what did they call that?"

Pablo: "A case of mistaken identity."

Grady: "That's it. Apparently the guy who lived here before him was who they were looking for. I guess he ran with a rough crowd and there's lots of people out there looking for him. But since that guy left the neighbors were so relieved. Then this poor guy and his family move in and got killed."

Pablo: <whispering to Grady> "Dad, I don't think you should say anything else."

Grady: "See, that's what's wrong with today's generation. They don't understand that we gotta look out for each other. Jose here knows what I'm talking about, right? You look like a hardworking man about my age. The owners are Mexican too and they look out for our people. They'll cut you a break when you need it, but you can't go telling everybody about it."

Pablo: "Dad!"

Rudy: "Was there a water leak in that bathroom?"

Grady: "Yes, but you're not supposed to be able to tell. What gave it away?"

Rudy: "The smell of mildew and the stain bleeding through the freshly painted wall and ceiling."

Grady: "Thanks for telling me. I know what to do to solve that problem. Call the owners and tell them you're interested in renting. If you become a tenant, maybe we can help each other out. I do all their maintenance repairs. If you need something special we can work something out. One hand washes the other. I keep telling them they should buy a new heater, the one they have now is outdated and keeps breaking down. They won't listen to me but if you moved in and kept complaining about it I bet you they'd have me install a new one."

Pablo: "Dad!"

Grady: "What? Calm down, Jose! These youngsters today, don't know when to be quiet. They don't have the wisdom of our years."

Discussion Questions:

1. Was Grady helpful or harmful to the landlords renting their place? Explain.
2. Was Grady intentionally making a racial slur by calling Rudy, Jose? Explain.
3. Can a member of the same protected class be in

violation of discrimination? Explain.

4. Would Grady be an employee you would proudly let interact with prospective tenants? Explain why or why not.

5. Did Grady and his son, Pablo, do anything as agents that are in violation of your company policies? Explain.

Follow-up Suggestions:

- Train your employees how to respond to prospects
- Have those you hire sign a Code of Conduct policy

Just for Fun:

A bus station is where a bus stops.
A train station is where a train stops.
On my desk, I have a work station...

       *   *   *

Friend1: "Why the long face?"

Friend2: "Three weeks ago my great-great grandfather who was extremely wealthy died. He left me one third of his fortune. Then last week a great aunt who I never met passed away and left me all her assets, she too had much wealth. Two weeks in a row this happened to me."

Friend1: "That is amazing. So why are you so glum? The loss caught up with you huh?"

Friend2: "No, nothing like that. It's the third week, and nothing has happened yet."

* Examine your perspective. Have you grown so skewed that your expectations are so high you fail to appreciate

all the good already present in your life?

*   *   *

That ye might walk worthy of the Lord unto all pleasing, being fruitful in every good work, and increasing in the knowledge of God;

Colossians 1:10 KJV

A Learning Stage 97 – A New Perspective in Black and White

Scenario:

Paul's niece, Sorrowful, calls his friend Jacob again for some needed advice.

Sorrowful: "Dude. I have this tenant who is a real pain. He does nothing but complain about everything. We have bent over backwards for this guy and nothing satisfies him. I've started ignoring his calls but my Uncle Paul said I need to respond. So I sent the jerk a letter and told him basically, *Dude, stop your whining. We can't afford to put you in the extravagant accommodations you are requesting. You're being a jerk. Knock it off. If you want all the stuff you're requesting done, do it yourself. Stop bothering me with your complaints I'm not your mother. If you don't like it, sue me!*"

Jacob: "Are any of the tenant's complaints reasonable and were they made in writing?"

Sorrowful: "No to the reasonable question, and once or twice in writing."

Jacob: "Give me some examples of his complaints."

Sorrowful: "Like, Dude, he called when we were out of town on vacation to say his power went out. He knew we weren't there. It turned out; some kids were playing a practical joke on Halloween and flipped the breaker switch. No big deal."

Jacob: "Actually, that is a big deal and a legitimate emergency. Go on."

Sorrowful: "Maybe so, but what about all the other times. He said the toilet seats were too small for him so my grandfather bought a larger toilet. Then he wanted the padded seat and we had it changed to accommodate him. Then the ceiling fans weren't giving him enough air so he demanded we pay for a new air conditioner. We purchased him a swamp cooler, he liked that so much we bought 2 more for two other rooms in his place. He claimed the smoke detectors were overly sensitive and he removed the batteries. Our maintenance crew said he admitted to smoking and the cigarette smoke was setting off the detectors. Then he complained about having ants and roaches. The exterminator was sent and said his living conditions, a messy environment were the contributing factors. He had food and dirty dishes lying around. We gave him and all the tenants a tip sheet and the exterminators gave a speech of how to avoid a pest problem. He was home but chose not to participate or attend."

Jacob: "Hear me out so I can get you to understand the importance of keeping your communications with tenants professional. He could walk into a courtroom and say, 'Judge my rental is a slum. I've asked for reasonable repairs and in return I got this nasty letter from my landlord who invites me to take up the court's time to sue him to get my repairs fixed. I don't ask for much, just electricity, air, a functional toilet, working smoke detectors and bug-free residence.' On the surface you can be made to sound like a slumlord and your responses thus far in writing will put a nail in your coffin. You need to show you took the repair requests seriously and took action in a timely manner. You went above and beyond but could not satisfy the tenant no matter what you did. An A/C was not an offered amenity and in your city is not required for habitability. However, you did offer ceiling fans and at your own expense provided a swamp cooler. Later when that appeased him somewhat, he demanded you provide two additional coolers at your expense. He disconnected smoke detectors which is a direct violation of his lease. He was smoking another violation of your "Smoke free addendum." According to the exterminator he was maintaining an unclean residence which caused only his apartment to have an insect infestation. You conducted a workshop with your exterminator company and all the tenants showed up except him. You sent out flyers to every tenant of how to avoid, detect and report the problem."

Sorrowful: "Dude, you explained that so cool. I like your examples. I get it now."

Sorrowful's Letter:
Dude, stop your whining. We can't afford to put you in the extravagant accommodations you are requesting. You're

being a jerk. Knock it off. If you want all the stuff you're requesting done, do it yourself. Stop bothering me with your complaints I'm not your mother. If you don't like it, sue me!"

Discussion Questions:

1. Analyze what Sorrowful said she wrote to the tenant. What issues could it raise?
2. "Stop whining. You're being a jerk, knock it off" can be interpreted to mean what?
3. Is it ever wise for a landlord to say he cannot afford to make a repair? Explain.
4. "Stop bothering me with your complaints" can give a judge in court what impression about Sorrowful as a landlord?
5. "If you don't like it, sue me!" is language a court may view in what way?
6. Did Sorrowful's letter refuse or imply that she would not take necessary action that was her responsibility? Explain.
7. What actions did Sorrowful take that showed she went above what was required of her as a landlord?
8. Why is it important to keep all communication on a business level?

Follow-up Suggestions:

- Keep all correspondences professional
- Do not make personal digs or attacks verbally or in writing
- Address the complaint with a business remedy
- Take swift action and document your follow up

- Rewrite Sorrowful's letter to read the way you think it should have been written

Just for Fun:

Question: What is the definition of the perfect Tenant?
Answer: The Landlord doesn't know what your name is.

*   *   *

Tenant Excuses For Not Paying The Rent
- "I can't pay my rent as my BMW is in the shop, and I cannot afford to pay for both."
- "I had my choice of paying the rent or buying a car. I bought a car. I knew you would understand."
- "I am sure I paid you -- YOU must have lost it."
- "You towed my car away that was illegally parked and I refuse to pay my rent until you get my car out of impound."
- "It's your fault. You deposited my check too late. My automatic withdrawals went through the bank before the rent check."
- "There is nowhere else to go. The place I applied to will not take me because you are evicting me."

*   *   *

My son, despise not the chastening of the LORD; neither be weary of his correction:
Proverbs 3:11 KJV
But he giveth more grace. Wherefore he saith, God resisteth the proud, but giveth grace unto the humble.
James 4:6 KJV

A Learning Stage 98 – Language Barriers

Have you experienced any dilemmas with applicants who do not speak or understand English? This is a growing problem that many landlords and managers face unsure of what is the best way to handle the problem.

<u>Scenario</u>:

~ Situation 1 ~

Judge1: "She says that she received a letter from you but did not understand it."

Landlord: "That's not my problem. These people need to learn to speak English."

Judge1: "She says all your prior dealings with her were in her native language."

Landlord: "That's a lie! I only speak English so that's not true. She's a liar, Judge."

Judge1: "Are you aware that the lease she signed with you is not in English?"

Landlord: "So what. I have the English version of it right here if you'd like to see it."

Judge1: "You just handed me a blank contract. This is not a contract she signed."

Landlord: "So what? We did her a favor because she said

she couldn't read or understand English. So we got a lease written up in her language to sign."

Judge1: "And what language were all the notices you sent out to her?"

Landlord: "English of course. It's the only language I speak. I've said that already."

Judge1: "Case dismissed."

~ Situation 2 ~

Judge2: "The dispute is over whether there is a breach of contract and cause to evict. The tenants say they were not told of any occupancy standard. They negotiated the lease with your agent in their language, which is not English. They signed an agreement that did not ask them how many occupants there were. And they were never given a copy of the contract in the language the contract was negotiated."

Landlord: "If you take a look, you see that all our contracts have a line to name all the intended occupants. We also require all adults to fill out separate applications."

Judge2: "Point that requirement out on the contract they signed."

Landlord: "I can't but I know my assistant explained it to them. She acquired an agreement in their language and had them fill it out. She then transferred their answers onto this lease and explained and translated the information. She filled out this English version for me, I required it, and had them sign it."

Judge2: "They say they were not asked for the names and number of occupants and it has not changed in the 18 months they have lived there. Where is the contract they initially filled out in their language, I didn't see it with your documents?"

Landlord: "I think my employee discarded it. We saw no reason to keep it."

Judge: "Is your employee here who spoke with them and translated everything to them, in court today?"

Landlord: "No. She left the business. We couldn't afford to keep another translator on staff, so we haven't hired any more since her. She couldn't make it today. But the contract is clear and they signed it. It does not list the seven people living there. So I don't understand why so much time is being spent on other issues."

Judge2: "Well, the only testimony I can rely on is of the witnesses present in court. And according to their testimony there is no subletting breach. You have been unable to prove they knowingly breached their initial contract, nor that they understood the notices you sent them in English. Case dismissed."

~ Situation 3 ~

DFEH: "I'm with the Department of Fair Employment and Housing and I am following up on a complaint we received. Would you give me your side please?"

Landlord: "He claims we treated him differently but we actually treated him better."

DFEH: "Did you ask his age, race, marital status, and number of children?"

Landlord: "No, I didn't. But aren't I entitled to that information if I want it?"

DFEH: "The application you gave him asked him for that information."

Landlord: "That's not my fault. The guy didn't speak English, so a friend of mine who has been a landlord for ages got me a copy of an application he uses for these people. I don't speak their language so how was I to know what the application asked for?"

DFEH: "Do you now see that using that application was not good?"

Landlord: "No, I don't. What I see is that no matter what I do you Fair Housing people are going to nitpick it to death and call it discrimination. If I had given him an English application knowing he didn't speak English, your organization would have criticized me. I go through the trouble of getting an application in his own language so he can read the thing to apply, even though dealing with these people takes up more of my time and energy, and I'm made to look like a villain. I'm here on the phone with you having to defend myself against an accusation of discrimination. What a waste of my valuable time, *again*."

DFEH: "Sir, we have a workshop coming up I suggest you and all your workers attend."

Landlord: "I'm not interested in filling your pockets with more of my money."

DFEH: "Sir, it is a free workshop and..."

Landlord: "I don't need a workshop to show me what a racket you crooks are running. I am going back to my original system and motto of, '*If you don't speak English, or look and act responsibly like me, I don't want you in my properties.*' I hope you're happy. You just ruined it for all the minorities and women with kids because I refuse to deal with them anymore. They're too much trouble. And I'm done talking to you too. If you want to talk to me again, contact my lawyer!"

The landlord slammed the phone down so hard, he broke it.

Discussion Questions:

1. Explain why the landlord's two cases were dismissed by the judges in detail.
2. What mistakes did the landlord make in each of the three situations?
3. What, if anything, did the landlord do right in the three situations?
4. What do you believe the Department of Fair Employment & Housing will do now?
5. Did the landlord say anything to DFEH that could be damaging to him? Explain.
6. Was the landlord's responses toward DFEH and the judge helpful? Explain.

Follow-up Suggestions:

- Review California Civil Code Section 1632 (Contract Law for Non-English Speaking Borrowers)
- Everyone must be given an equal opportunity to apply and rent your property
- You are not required to provide forms in any language other than English
- If you choose to supply documents in a language you are not fluent in, you open yourself up to problematic issues

- Always consult a qualified attorney should you have any legal questions
- Speak with a qualified Fair Housing representative if you are confused on what matters they consider violations
- Attend training regularly to keep yourself informed
- Do not use documents you are unable to understand and translate yourself

Just for Fun:

Question: What do honest lawyers and UFOs have in common?

Answer: You always hear about them, but you never see them.

*   *   *

Study to shew thyself approved unto God, a workman that needeth not to be ashamed, rightly dividing the word of truth.

2 Timothy 2:15 KJV

And they that have believing masters, let them not despise [them], because they are brethren; but rather do [them] service, because they are faithful and beloved, partakers of the benefit. These things teach and exhort.

1 Timothy 6:2 KJV

A Learning Stage 99 – Advice of Contradiction

A prospective applicant was skeptical about applying so questions were posed to the manager before enduring the screening process.

Applicant: "I would like to apply for your rental but I don't want to waste my money paying a screening fee if I'm just going to be denied."

Manager: "I recommend you look at our criteria and review our Application Procedure to help you self-qualify, to make a conscious decision."

Applicant: "I looked it over. I have good credit, good rental history and I qualify. However, you say you'll only accept service animals. I don't know what that is. I don't have one of those, but I have a comfort pet."

Manager: "Oh, I don't know what that is? Is the pet to accommodate a disability?"

Applicant: "Yes."

Manager: "Okay, what kind of pet is it?"

Applicant: "A pit bull."

Manager: "Oh, my! I tell you what, I'm not sure about that. I'll look into it and get back to you."

The manager immediately called the landlord and informed him of the situation. Initially the landlord reluctantly began to bend when told it was an accommodation, but reversed back to being resistant upon finding that the animal was a pit bull. The landlord looked in the yellow pages for an attorney.

*

~ First inquiry by the landlord ~

Attorney: "You do have a dilemma. I'd be glad to set an appointment for you to come in and discuss the matter further. You'll only have to pay a small consultation fee."

*

~ Second inquiry by the landlord ~

Secretary2: "Attorney Shark has handled cases like that before, she knows what to do. You can come speak with her in person and she can advise you on this."

Landlord: "I just want a straight answer to my question. If I go down there, is there a fee?"

Secretary2: "Yes, there is a consultation fee."

Landlord: "And I'll have to wait, and fill out forms and such...I know the drill. When can I come in?"

Secretary2: "She has an opening next Wednesday."

Landlord: "What? No I can't wait that long."

Secretary2: "You can post the question on our online website and pay the fee with a major credit card and have your question answered within 48 hours."

*

~ Third inquiry by the landlord ~

Attorney2: "Pit bull? No, I would deny the application. But before I did, I'd contact my insurance agent. Look at your contract, because normally some companies will cancel your insurance if you allow an animal like that on the premises."

Landlord: "That's true. I hadn't thought about that. You have been so helpful."

*

~The landlord called his insurance company~

Agent: "If you allow a pit bull as a pet it will force us to cancel your coverage with us."

Landlord: "Thank you, that's all I need to hear."

~ The manager also decided to investigate further ~

Manager: "You are a member of an apartment association you're always raving about and attend training classes, what do you think?"

Friend: "You have to accept the animal, as long as they comply with the law making the request. The applicant has to provide written authorization from a reputable and verifiable person to attest to the need for the accommodation. If it does not present a hardship on you that you can prove – which is hard to do, so don't even try that avenue if it's not true – then you must allow the accommodation. Call Fair Housing and go online onto their website and see what they say about this."

~ The manager called and spoke with Fair Housing ~

Fair Housing: "The applicant must make the request in writing and give you written authorization from a medical doctor that the pit bull is needed."

A LEARNING STAGE 3

~ The manager telephoned the applicant with an update ~

Manager: "You have to request the accommodation in writing and provide medical documentation in writing from a doctor."

Applicant: "I don't have that, but I do have a letter from my social worker."

Manager: "I don't think that will be sufficient but I'll tell the owner and see what he wants to do."

~ The manager and landlord compared notes ~

Landlord: "Deny the application. We don't allow pets unless they're service animals. I hear those comfort pets are usually bogus but I talked to attorneys and my insurance. The attorneys either wanted money upfront, wanted me to fill out forms, or said I had to set an appointment to come down and ask the question. One guy was nice and I trust him. He's the one who referred me to my insurance company and told me I could deny the pit bull. And he gave me this advice free and didn't charge me for it. I trust him. Sure enough my insurance threatens to cancel me if I permit that pit bull as a pet."

Manager: "My friend said we had to accept it and she goes to training a lot. But she also told me to call Fair Housing and check their website."

Landlord: "Yes, but you also said Fair Housing told you he had to get a report from a medical doctor and he only had something from a social worker. A social worker is not a medical doctor."

Manager: "I know but I still feel uneasy about it. I'd like to know why my friend was so adamant about accepting the animal."

Landlord: "Frankly, I don't care. I've made my decision and I have the support of an attorney, my insurance company and Fair Housing from what you've said. I'm not wasting any more time on this."

~ The manager contacted her friend a second time ~

Friend: "It is recommended the request be put in writing but it isn't mandatory. A social worker qualifies as a reliable party to write an authorization and you have the right to verify the social worker and that he or she wrote the note. You have little to no say as to the type of companion animal. With the exception of someone who wants to bring in an animal that is illegal or dangerous. Like they can't bring a lion, endangered species, elephant...nothing outrageous or unreasonable."

The applicant was denied tenancy and reported the matter to Fair Housing. Fair Housing tried to mediate and instructed the manager to make the accommodation. The landlord refused and a lawsuit was filed against him. The landlord was ultimately fined and both he and the manager had to pay to attend Fair Housing training.

Follow-up Suggestions:

- Find out what the law says on the matter
- Acquire documentation to support your action
- Carefully consider who wrote the document

- Is there a more current or superseding document?
- Was the document you are relying on composed by Fair Housing, DOJ, HUD in Washington D.C., Sacramento, or in your state/region?
- When you receive advice that is contradictory, find a safe solution

<u>Just for Fun:</u>

THINGS YOU DON'T WANT TO SEE ON YOUR EMPLOYEE EVALUATION
- "His men would follow him anywhere, but only out of morbid curiosity."
- "This employee is really not so much of a has-been, but more of a definitely won't be."
- "Works well when under constant supervision and cornered like a rat in a trap."
- "When she opens her mouth, it seems that this is only to change whichever foot was previously in there."
- "He would be out of his depth in a parking lot puddle."
- "She sets low personal standards and then consistently fails to achieve them."

*   *   *

My brethren, be not many masters, knowing that we shall receive the greater condemnation.
James 3:1 KJV

A Learning Stage 100 – Final Exam

See if you can answer the questions correctly from memory before searching for the answers.

1. All landlords are required to commit to a 2+1 occupancy standard?
   A. True
   B. False

2. It is illegal to question any person listed on an applicant's application, unless they are listed as a reference?
   A. True
   B. False

3. What are 4 of the 10 ways you can avoid being a test case for a discrimination lawsuit?

4. Does an Application Procedure and Selection Criteria have to be in writing? Explain why or why not.

5. When is the best time to turn over keys to the rental and grant a new applicant access?

6. Who should you permit to show a prospective tenant your vacancy?

7. What are 5 things landlords want from vendors they hire?

8. Are there things you can do to reduce disputes and minimize misunderstandings should you decide to rent to a friend or relative? Explain.

9. If you hear rumors that your tenants are doing something illegal in your rental, should you enter the rental when you believe no one is home to gather evidence? Explain.

10. Is it important for landlords to receive ongoing training? Explain.

11. How many current issues can you list that have recently been legislated and have greatly impacted the rental industry and how landlords operate their business?

12. If someone requests a disabled variance and appears to qualify but you have suspicions that they are attempting to dupe you, should you deny their request? Explain.

13. Would it be okay to secretly give preferential treatment to some tenants you do not allow others to have? For example waiving a late fee for a single mother but charging a single guy the late fee without hesitation.

14. Must a landlord endure hearing tenant complaints? Is it wise to notify a tenant in writing, who is current on their rent, to stop bothering you with ridiculous complaints?

15. Should a landlord who speaks only English ever supply rental documents in another language for an applicant's convenience? Why or why not?

16. Pick a scripture you would like to model your business practices after.

17. What should a landlord do when receiving conflicting information from experts?

18. Prepare a list for a team of professionals you might need to seek advice from.

19. What can a landlord do to hone his skills and stay informed?

20. Name four areas that can reveal impropriety in your business.

Follow-up Suggestions:

Owning and managing rental property can be an overwhelming job. To simplify the copious documents and forms used I recommend five of the basics that provide you with a good foundation for your business.

All your forms should conform to be two things:

1 – up to date and
2 – in a language you understand

* Please also review California Civil Code Section 1632 (Contract Law for Non-English Speaking Borrowers) or research the statutes in your state that regulate your contracts.

5 Documents that should be used with each tenancy transaction:
- Application
- Application Procedure
- Selection Criteria
- Month-to-month rental agreement or lease
- Move-in/Move-out checklist

Important pamphlet:
- EPA's booklet "Protect Your Family From Lead In Your Home" or "The Lead-Safe Certified Guide to Renovate Right" (*for rentals built pre-1978*)

7 Frequently used addendums:
- Pet Addendum
- Bed Bug Addendum
- Satellite Dish Addendum
- Disability Variance Form
- Crime-Free Addendum
- "Owner/Agent Acknowledgement of Resident(s) Thirty-Day Notice of Intent to Vacate" & "Notice of Resident Option to Request Initial Inspection of the Rental Unit" forms

Just for Fun:

Silly Court Questions
Attorney: What is your date of birth sir?
Witness: July 17th.
Attorney: What year?
Witness: Every year.

*   *   *

Attorney: Remember all your responses must be oral. OK? Now, what school do you go to?
Witness: Oral.
Attorney: How old are you?
Witness: Oral.

*   *   *

Attorney: Doctor, how many autopsies have you performed on dead people?
Witness: All my autopsies have been performed on dead people.

*   *   *

And the Lord answered me, and said, Write the vision, and make it plain upon tables, that he may run that readeth it.
Habakkuk 2:2 KJV
For which of you, intending to build a tower, sitteth not down first, and counteth the cost, whether he have sufficient to finish it?
Luke 14:28 KJV

A Learning Stage 101 – The Test of Time

If you handle each tenant the same per your policies, there is less room for discrimination claims. As long as your rules are legal and in line with enforcing agencies, and followed.

<u>Scenario</u>:

Jacob: "Paul, how are you? This is Jacob from All Estate Management."

Paul: "Well, this is a first. I'm usually the one calling you."

Jacob: "I had to call to say I received your check in the mail, thank you."

Paul: "I just wanted to pay it forward, for someone else to attend your training. That repair policy addendum you gave me helped me out a lot. I had all my tenants sign the form and not a moment too soon. A few months later, a fairly new tenant lost his job. Instead of going about it responsibly, they stopped paying rent. I sent them a three day notice and they responded on the third day. I accepted a partial payment, updated the amount owed and as a receipt I gave them a new three day notice for the balance. I later was informed by another tenant that the code enforcement and health department were called to complain about habitability issues after I started the eviction process in court."

Jacob: "That's what I'd been hearing tenants were doing to cause problems for landlords. This is a way of excusing why they stopped paying rent. Most of the issues they complain about, they purposely cause, giving agencies reason to inspect."

Paul: "Everything that judge asked for, I was ready to present. I even surprised myself. I did what you've been telling me, to 'let my documented proof do most of the talking.' They admitted they had not paid but said it was because of repairs I didn't take care of and habitability issues. I presented move-in photos and checklists they signed, showing that there were no issues. I showed the repair policy the tenants signed, my repair log documenting a pattern of how quickly I respond to repair requests. I argued I never received any requests from them and their calling outside agencies without contacting me first was a direct violation of our contract."

Jacob: "Wow Paul, my how you've grown. How did the judge respond?"

Paul: "He not only gave me possession back, but awarded me every penny I asked for. I've never had a court case go that well for me. And I didn't need to hire an attorney, so there were no legal expenses."

Jacob: "What? You really have matured in this business. I thought you started using a management company that used a good law firm on all your court actions."

Paul: "I did, because I was afraid to make a mistake and lose cases. But my take-away value from your training workshop and retreat gave me a new way of thinking. If I have situations that may involve some tricky issues, I'll hire an experienced and qualified lawyer. But for the most part, because of all I've learned, I haven't needed it anymore. I changed my documents and screen prospects more efficiently, form and enforce legally-sound policies, and handle matters that clearly demonstrate fair and equal treatment. As a result, professional tenants are deterred, I avoid committing Fair Housing violations, I retain good tenants, and drastically reduce court actions."

Discussion Questions:

1. When is it best to retain an attorney to represent you in court?
2. What evidence can help you defend against an inhabitability claim?
3. Had Paul not presented his case well, what could have happened?
4. How long could it have taken to get these tenants out?
5. Since the tenants stopped paying rent, then called enforcement agencies to try to stay, could Paul have constructively evicted them for calling? Explain.
6. What significance, if any at all, did non-payment of rent and the timing the tenants raised inhabitability claims have on showing the tenants' motives? How? Explain.

7. Would you have accepted a partial payment? Why or why not?
8. If a landlord accepts money after serving a notice, list the steps that must be taken afterwards to preserve his/her rights.

Follow-up Suggestions:

- Keep good records
- Conduct regular inspections
- Compose and enforce a repair policy
- Attend training as often as you can
- Surround yourself with your peers on a regular basis, and learn from their experiences

Just for Fun:

Q: What is the difference concerning a catfish and an attorney?
A: One is a scum-sucking bottom feeder, and the other is a catfish.

*   *   *

Silly Court Questions
Attorney: This Myasthenia Gavis, does it affect your memory at all?
Witness: Yes.
Attorney: And in what ways does it affect your memory?
Witness: I forget things.
Attorney: You forget things? Can you give us an example of something you've forgotten?

*   *   *

Where no counsel is, the people fall: but in the multitude of counsellors there is safety.
Proverbs 11:14 KJV

Expert Query Log

Consider keeping a log of training you attended, important lessons you learned, where you acquired the information, who taught you and how you may contact them in the future. Below is simply a draft sample. You are welcome to create and adapt your own log and cater it to your needs. I recommend you update this annually.

Some subjects to keep in mind and incorporate in your list could be advertising tips, tenant screening advice, questions/comments permissible to ask applicants, resident criteria, new laws, housing violations, legal updates, and inquiries you plan to ask an attorney or expert at an upcoming workshop or class.

Fair Housing
1. Phone number _____
2. Person you spoke with _____
3. Job title _____
4. Date _____ Time _____
5. Next available workshop you registered to attend
   _____
6. Notes: _____
   _____

TERESA BILLINGSLEY

_____
_____
_____
_____
_____
_____
_____
_____
_____
_____
_____
_____
_____
_____
_____
_____
_____

Landlord/Tenant Attorney
1. Phone number _____
2. Person you spoke with _____
3. Job title _____
4. Date _____ Time _____
5. Next available workshop you registered to attend
_____
6. Notes: _____
_____
_____
_____
_____
_____
_____

A LEARNING STAGE 3

_____
_____
_____
_____
_____
_____
_____
_____
_____
_____
_____
_____
_____
_____
_____

Rental Expert
1. Phone number _____
2. Person you spoke with _____
3. Job title _____
4. Date _____ Time _____
5. Next available workshop you registered to attend
   _____
6. Notes: _____
_____
_____
_____
_____
_____
_____
_____
_____
_____

_____
_____
_____
_____
_____
_____
_____
_____
_____
_____
_____
_____

Websites:

Documents:

Helpful Resources:

A LEARNING STAGE 3

Names & Phone Numbers of other experts:

Training you attended this year:

Books/Articles/Laws you read that educated you & are handy to have:

People you shared rental updates with:

Potential Vendors:

Networking Circle:

<u>Just for Fun:</u>

Silly Court Questions
Attorney: Now doctor -- Isn't it true that when a person dies in his sleep, in most cases, he just passes quietly away and doesn't know anything about it until the next morning?

*   *   *

Attorney: Were you alone or by yourself?

*   *   *

And the Lord answered me, and said, Write the vision, and make it plain upon tables, that he may run that readeth it.
Habakkuk 2:2 KJV
For which of you, intending to build a tower, sitteth not down first, and counteth the cost, whether he have sufficient to finish it?
Luke 14:28 KJV

10 Property Management Repair Alerts

There are reputable management companies that operate with ethical standards. For the many that do not, a rental property owner should beware of some ongoing behavior being displayed to extort money from them with repairs. One company was so egregious they resorted to all ten of these tactics at an expense of over $16,000 for alleged, unsubstantiated, unnecessary and unauthorized repairs that rarely resulted in a resolution. I saved over $30,000 by having reliable professionals assess the repairs, solve the problem or honor their warranties. These are 10 common repair situations rental property owners should look out for.

1 - Create a sense of urgency

When the repair is made to seem urgent it limits your abilities to investigate. The repair is relayed as a safety or habitability issue. Or the maintenance worker is said to be on site, ready to make the repair. If he is not authorized to do the job and has to leave or be called back, service fees are said to apply.

Occasionally this may be legitimate. Be on guard if this

becomes a pattern. Beware of frequent calls where management hinders you from having time to consider a second opinion or utilizing your own trusted vendors.

2 - Double dip

This is when you are charged more than once for the same fix.

I authorized 2 hours to finalize a repair by their maintenance crew. I was later told they could not spare the manpower and called an expert vendor to handle it. Management later billed me for the expert who did the job and the following month, charges were noted for their staff to perform the same job.

3 - Pocket a secret commission

They tell you the project was done at a precise cost, but continuously avoid producing an invoice.

I was able to acquire one invoice that showed their vendor charged $600 less than what I was told and the management company pocketed the difference.

4 - Overcharge

I was told a repair would cost $2800. An inquiry of a different supervisor contradicted the other, saying the vendor requested $2150.

I spoke to and paid the vendor directly and the price was indeed $2150. Had I not intervened, past dealings *indicate $2800 would have been deducted from my account and management would have taken $650 for themselves.*

5 - Exceed authority racking up unauthorized charges

Management contracts typically have at least a paragraph or section that addresses how repairs and maintenance issues are to be handled. This is so that parties can prevent common misunderstandings, scams, and problems pervasive in the industry. There is a reason to be suspicious of any management company that knowingly operates outside the parameters of your written contract at great expense to you.

I received an urgent call that an emergent plumbing problem had presented itself, tenants had to be evacuated and major repair work done. Management needed my approval to call their expert vendor to finish the job. I later discovered from the billing records, that they had been billing and responding to this alleged problem for some time. They first notified me after they had already accumulated approximately 5 days, over 20 hours of their staff time and 1 day of holiday/afterhours pay for their expert vendor. They failed to provide me with accurate information to make an informed decision on using a company to assess and cure the problem in a sensible manner.

6 - No invoices

Good business involves documentation. Blind trust is

foolish, especially when it has not been earned. There is no valid reason for a company not to produce written records and a cohesive account of expenses.

7 - Untimely charges showing up weeks or months after the alleged job was done

There should be no surprises and questionable entries on your regular statements.

I had paid for services and later noticed separate charges noted for materials that I was unfamiliar with. I was unable to get answers from management. I asked a contractor what the items listed were for. I discovered they were plumbing parts, but no plumbing repairs had been made for over 2 months. These sneaky insertions often elude the average rental property owner because most fail to review their statements and verify the accuracy of each notation.

8 - Additional stringent contingencies placed upon outside vendors you refer to management

Most workers want to show up on the job, evaluate it, make the repair, get paid and move on to the next project. If they have to go out of their way to a management company to pick up and return a key, wait, sign in, produce their driver's license, fill out an application, list the management as an additional insured on their insurance policy, have $2 million liability coverage and show management proof and be told once they arrive that they will have to come back another day because management is not prepared and cannot find the key, it nearly guarantees them a monopoly on repairs. No worker will endure such stipulations; or they will require a major increase in payment to put up with these alarming prerequisites.

9 - Repeat charges for work that does not resolve the alleged issue

You may receive a call for the first repair. It is explained to your satisfaction and you consent to the job and fee amount. When you get your statement, the charge you okayed is there along with another fee shortly thereafter for the same job.

Rather than call me, management elected to pay their referred company a second time at my expense because the first visit did not fix the issue. Good representation would have held their vendor accountable, informed me of the situation, or gotten a refund and utilized the money to hire another company to do the job correctly.

10 - Refusal to enforce active warranties

Rather than enforcing active warranties, management makes a conscious decision to suggest you hire their vendors at an inflated rate.

To get an unbiased opinion, I called a company I had never done business with for a free evaluation and assessment. Management met with them and provided access. The worker called me with a warning. He immediately noticed it was a new install and suggested I implement the warranty. My management was trying to *have me approve another new install at $11,000+ and all other professionals concurred this was not necessary.*

Use your best judgment and do not ignore your intuition. It is possible for management to make errors and it is not beneficial to assume a mistake is an intentional act to scam you. Bring up any problems as soon as they are realized and afford management an opportunity to explain and correct. The way they respond or their failure to act will give you a better indication of whether they acted inadvertently in error or whether it was intentional to defraud you. For legal advice, consult a qualified attorney.

4 Tangible Clues That Reveal Impropriety in Business

Where should you look for clues of impropriety? No one wants to believe the person you chose to be in business with is being disloyal. When red flags pop up consistently, it's time to examine four areas that will help you determine if there is unscrupulous behavior or simply a misunderstanding of events that need clarification.

If you perceive cheating in your business, avoid jumping to conclusions and give the other party an opportunity to clear up any suspicions you have. When the response is defensive, does not make sense or you are put off or ignored so they can stall, it is a bad sign. Most people who have nothing to hide are forthcoming and immediately want to correct errors to restore trust. When someone avoids answering you and dodges legitimate business inquiries, it is often an indication they know they are guilty of misdealing, and hope to misdirect your focus onto other matters to delay or pacify you into forgetting about the issue and letting it go.

Questioning the person directly is not your only option. It is simply a necessary step before coming to any conclusions. People deserve the benefit of the doubt and an opportunity to give their side of things. However, when they refuse to take the chance to explain themselves then look into areas that will provide you with undisputed and tangible evidence. There are 4 areas that usually will give you clues and reveal whether or not there is impropriety within your organization.

1. Financials
- Income – are all the proper funds being collected and accounted for?
- Expenses – are they all legitimate, necessary and agreed upon?
- Balances – are the dollar amounts reflecting an accurate balance each time?
- Reports and Records – do they reflect outstanding and unexplained missing funds?

2. Policy violations
- Have there been incidents where the other party has acted outside of the rules and policies they promised to uphold and abide by?
- Are they fulfilling their duties?
- Have you noticed negligence in the performance of services they are to provide?
- Do they create liability situations for you?
- Can you prove that ethical infractions have been committed?
- Are decisions being made beyond your best interests that fail to protect you and your investment?

3. Paperwork and Documentation
- Are written reports clear?
- Does reviewing the reports provide you with a full picture of how your business is doing?

- Have you noticed so many insertions that you are dissuaded from perusing them in depth?

4. Integrity faux paux-es/Suspicious Reporting
- Can you rely on what is reported to you?
- Were there times you have caught them in lies?
- When you have communications with them, is there a sense of relief that you are in business with the right people?
- Do you feel on guard and a loss of trust each time they make a statement to you?

If you scrutinize the above four areas, it will often provide you with the required information to determine whether or not there is a problem that needs to be addressed.

16 Signs of a Bitter vs. Better Employee

According to an article, *Property Management & Employee Turnover*, "Industry surveys show that turnover is particularly high within the property management field." Also, "It costs companies a minimum of $10,000 per employee and exceeds $30,000 to find and train replacements for each lost worker." This article was written by Emily Beach and may be read in its entirety at http://smallbusiness.chron.com/property-management-employee-turnover-13312.html.

As an employee, you are the gatekeeper of the organization. Consumers do not customarily see the owners, they see you. You represent all the company stands for. So, remember all the positive things you mentioned in your interview about why you wanted to work specifically for this particular corporation for future reference.

Now that you were lucky enough to have sold yourself into being hired, it is time to live up to your duties. Fulfill and honor the ethical standards you signed on for. Do not become bitter that you are expected to honor and perform tasks that are not always desirable and may often be unappreciated. There is no excuse for becoming disgruntled and staying in the job, making everyone around you miserable. You are not entitled to inflict your poor attitude onto consumers nor infect the mood of your co-workers.

If you are uncertain which category you fall in, here are some clues that distinguish between a bitter and a better employee.

A Bitter Employee:

1. Complains about the problems within the company
2. Badmouths the weaknesses of the establishment
3. Criticizes what others are doing wrong that they say bring the business down
4. Abandons the job if they fail to receive the degree of accolades they believe is due them
5. Seeks their own praise and glory
6. Puts in less effort when they feel they are not properly rewarded for their performance
7. Will gossip about the flaws in their job to other employees and potential consumers
8. Wants to personally succeed
9. Constantly scrutinizes what else the company can do for them
10. Dreads coming to work where they feel unappreciated for doing work they must force themselves to do
11. Frequently seek some type of compensation for every task they complete
12. Only exerts a level of performance they believe the company is paying them for
13. Feels powerless and will take out their frustration on

clients and other staff members
14. Are silent when others are mistreated but speak out vehemently for themselves when they feel wronged
15. Care only about themselves and what is in it for them
16. Think their abilities and work product are above their pay grade

<u>A Better Employee</u>:

1. Will make suggestions to promote the efficiency of the company
2. Highlights the good and positive aspects of the organization
3. Offers their own gifts and talents to improve productivity
4. Remains loyal and dedicated and continues to do what they can to make the company shine
5. Are motivated to uplift the company and raise its reputation to a higher level
6. Feel privileged they were hired and honored to receive pay for work they enjoy doing
7. Will only speak of the attributes and strengths of their employer to others. Never reveals potential liabilities unless to those in charge and in private, along with viable options on ways to resolve the problems
8. Desires to be instrumental in the success of the organization
9. Persistently self-evaluates and looks for opportunities to do more for their employer
10. Looks forward to coming to work to provide a service in their chosen field
11. Do not keep score and gladly give their full efforts on the job at all times

12. Are committed and dedicated to a fault
    - *You must watch this and ensure other important areas of your life are not sacrificed unnecessarily and lost – family, fun, faith, health*
13. Do not see themself as a victim and are vocal about advocating for both customers and their institution
14. Are more passionate fighting for the rights of others than for themselves
15. Have concerns that are primarily focused on what they can do for others
16. Are appreciative and take advantage of every training opportunity. Feel eager to grow, honored to benefit from hands-on experience and welcome chances to hone their craft

It is critical to ones survival to have balance. A *better* employee can be misused by employers who exploit their loyalties, if allowed. It is incumbent upon the employee to set boundaries. Learn to negotiate and do your best to work with your employer.

Employers must be more diligent in their efforts to recognize their *better* employees. Do your best to work with them to maintain their employ. Business savvy bosses will go out of their way to keep valued workers. It is simply a wise decision and makes good business sense.

Bitter employees are not bad people. They are often misunderstood and misplaced. They have not found their niche. Those who are busy working at what they love find little time to be bitter. A challenge I hope employers will accept is to recognize the needs of *bitter* employees and help turn them into *better* ones.

MORE HELPFUL SCRIPTURES

More Helpful Scriptures

These are scriptures I did not use but would like to recommend you consider as good references.

Get wisdom and prepare yourself well
And unto one he gave five talents, to another two, and to another one; to every man according to his several ability; and straightway took his journey.

Matthew 25:15 KJV

Happy *is* the man *that* findeth wisdom, and the man *that* getteth understanding.

Proverbs 3:13 KJV

(11) Not that I speak in respect of want: for I have learned, in whatsoever state I am, *therewith* to be content.

(12) I know both how to be abased, and I know how to abound: every where and in all things I am instructed both to be full and to be hungry, both to abound and to suffer need.

(13) I can do all things through Christ which strengtheneth me.

Philippians 4:11-13 KJV

(24) Therefore whosoever heareth these sayings of mine, and doeth them, I will liken him unto a wise man, which

built his house upon a rock:

(25) And the rain descended, and the floods came, and the winds blew, and beat upon that house; and it fell not: for it was founded upon a rock.

(26) And every one that heareth these sayings of mine, and doeth them not, shall be likened unto a foolish man, which built his house upon the sand:

(27) And the rain descended, and the floods came, and the winds blew, and beat upon that house; and it fell: and great was the fall of it.

Matthew 7:24-27 KJV

Learn to speak with wisdom or be silent

To every *thing there is* a season, and a time to every purpose under the heaven:

Ecclesiastes 3:1 KJV

A time to rend, and a time to sew; a time to keep silence, and a time to speak;

Ecclesiastes 3:7 KJV

Then he questioned with him in many words; but he answered him nothing.

Luke 23:9 KJV

Therefore the prudent shall keep silence in that time; for it *is* an evil time.

Amos 5:13 KJV

In the multitude of words there wanteth not sin: but he that refraineth his lips *is* wise.

Proverbs 10:19 KJV

And they could not take hold of his words before the people: and they marvelled at his answer, and held their peace.

Luke 20:26 KJV

(4) And Pilate asked him again, saying, Answerest thou

226

nothing? behold how many things they witness against thee.

(5) But Jesus yet answered nothing; so that Pilate marvelled.

Mark 15:4-5 KJV

The LORD shall fight for you, and ye shall hold your peace.

Exodus 14:14 KJV

O that ye would altogether hold your peace! and it should be your wisdom.

Job 13:5 KJV

He that is void of wisdom despiseth his neighbour: but a man of understanding holdeth his peace.

Proverbs 11:12 KJV

(1) A soft answer turneth away wrath: but grievous words stir up anger.

(2) The tongue of the wise useth knowledge aright: but the mouth of fools poureth out foolishness.

Proverbs 15:1-2 KJV

Obey the law and treat people respectfully

(13) Submit yourselves to every ordinance of man for the Lord's sake: whether it be to the king, as supreme;

(14) Or unto governors, as unto them that are sent by him for the punishment of evildoers, and for the praise of them that do well.

(15) For so is the will of God, that with well doing ye may put to silence the ignorance of foolish men:

(17) Honour all *men*. Love the brotherhood. Fear God. Honor the king.

(18) Servants, *be* subject to *your* masters with all fear, not only to the good and gentle, but also to the froward.

I Peter 2:13-15, 17-18 KJV

And he said unto them, Render therefore unto Caesar the things which be Caesar's, and unto God the things which be God's.

Luke 20:25 KJV

Strive not with a man without cause, if he have done thee no harm.

Proverbs 3:30 KJV

Those blessed to be in charge have a duty not to abuse their position

Now we know that what things soever the law saith, it saith to them who are under the law: that every mouth may be stopped, and all the world may become guilty before God.

Romans 3:19 KJV

But he that knew not, and did commit things worthy of stripes, shall be beaten with few *stripes*. For unto whomsoever much is given, of him shall be much required: and to whom men have committed much, of him they will ask the more.

Luke 12:48 KJV

And the King shall answer and say unto them, Verily I say unto you, Inasmuch as ye have done it unto one of the least of these my brethren, ye have done it unto me.

Matthew 25:40 KJV

He that oppresseth the poor reproacheth his Maker: but he that honoureth him hath mercy on the poor.

Proverbs 14:31 KJV

Withhold not good from them to whom it is due, when it is in the power of thine hand to do *it*.

Proverbs 3:27 KJV

(23) Thus saith the Lord, Let not the wise *man* glory in his wisdom, neither let the mighty *man* glory in his might, let

not the rich *man* glory in his riches:

(24) But let him that glorieth glory in this, that he understandeth and knoweth me, that I *am* the Lord which exercise lovingkindness, judgment, and righteousness, in the earth: for in these *things* I delight, saith the Lord.

Jeremiah 9:23-24 KJV

Options when you do not know what to do

(6) Be careful for nothing; but in every thing by prayer and supplication with thanksgiving let your requests be made known unto God.

(7) And the peace of God, which passeth all understanding, shall keep your hearts and minds through Christ Jesus.

(8) Finally, brethren, whatsoever things are true, whatsoever things *are* honest, whatsoever things *are* just, whatsoever things *are* pure, whatsoever things *are* lovely, whatsoever things *are* of good report; if *there be* any virtue, and if *there be* any praise, think on these things.

(9) Those things, which ye have both learned, and received, and heard, and seen in me, do: and the God of peace shall be with you.

Philippians 4:6-9 KJV

If my people, which are called by my name, shall humble themselves, and pray, and seek my face, and turn from their wicked ways; then will I hear from heaven, and will forgive their sin, and will heal their land.

2 Chronicles 7:14 KJV

Who is wise, and he shall understand these *things*? prudent, and he shall know them? for the ways of the Lord *are* right, and the just shall walk in them: but the transgressors shall fall therein.

Hosea 14:9 KJV

God is a trustworthy and reliable source so do not give up or lose hope

(5) Trust in the LORD with all thine heart; and lean not unto thine own understanding.

(6) In all thy ways acknowledge him, and he shall direct thy paths.

(7) Be not wise in thine own eyes: fear the Lord, and depart from evil.

Proverbs 3:5-7 KJV

(28) Hast thou not known? hast thou not heard, *that* the everlasting God, the LORD, the Creator of the ends of the earth, fainteth not, neither is weary? *there is* no searching of his understanding.

(29) He giveth power to the faint; and to *them that have* no might he increaseth strength.

(30) Even the youths shall faint and be weary, and the young men shall utterly fall:

(31) But they that wait upon the LORD shall renew *their* strength; they shall mount up with wings as eagles; they shall run, and not be weary; *and* they shall walk, and not faint.

Isaiah 40:28-31 KJV

He shall not be afraid of evil tidings: his heart is fixed, trusting in the LORD.

Psalm 112:7 KJV

But my God shall supply all your need according to his riches in glory by Christ Jesus.

Philippians 4:19 KJV

For we are the circumcision, which worship God in the spirit, and rejoice in Christ Jesus, and have no confidence in the flesh.

Philippians 3:3 KJV

There is no wisdom nor understanding nor counsel against the Lord.

Proverbs 21:30 KJV

Keep honing your craft

Therefore we ought to give the more earnest heed to the things which we have heard, lest at any time we should let *them* slip.

Hebrews 2:1 KJV

(1) But speak thou the things which become sound doctrine:

(8) Sound speech, that cannot be condemned; that he that is of the contrary part may be ashamed, having no evil thing to say of you.

(15) These things speak, and exhort, and rebuke with all authority. Let no man despise thee.

Titus 2:1, 8, 15 KJV

Put them in mind to be subject to principalities and powers, to obey magistrates, to be ready to every good work,

Titus 3:1 KJV

Charge them that are rich in this world, that they be not highminded, nor trust in uncertain riches, but in the living God, who giveth us richly all things to enjoy;

1Timothy 6:17 KJV

Wherefore the rather, brethren, give diligence to make your calling and election sure: for if ye do these things, ye shall never fall:

2 Peter 1:10 KJV

Accept instruction and correction

For the commandment *is* a lamp; and the law *is* light; and reproofs of instruction *are* the way of life:

Proverbs 6:23 KJV

231

(8) All the words of my mouth *are* in righteousness; *there is* nothing froward or perverse in them.

(9) They *are* all plain to him that understandeth, and right to them that find knowledge.

(32) Now therefore hearken unto me, O ye children: for blessed *are they that* keep my ways.

(33) Hear instruction, and be wise, and refuse it not.

Proverbs 8:8-9, 32-33 KJV

For whom the LORD loveth he correcteth; even as a father the son *in whom* he delighteth.

Proverbs 3:12 KJV

A scorner loveth not one that reproveth him: neither will he go unto the wise.

Proverbs 15:12 KJV

Plans go wrong for lack of advice; many counselors bring success.

Proverbs 15:22 NLT

(31) The ear that heareth the reproof of life abideth among the wise.

(32) He that refuseth instruction despiseth his own soul: but he that heareth reproof getteth understanding.

(33) The fear of the Lord is the instruction of wisdom; and before honour is humility.

Proverbs 15:31-33 KJV

(8) The wise in heart will receive commandments: but a prating fool shall fall.

(17) He *is in* the way of life that keepeth instruction: but he that refuseth reproof erreth.

Proverbs 10:8, 17 KJV

There is reward for hard work and due diligence

He becometh poor that dealeth *with* a slack hand: but the hand of the diligent maketh rich.

Proverbs 10:4 KJV

Where no oxen *are*, the crib *is* clean: but much increase *is* by the strength of the ox.

Proverbs 14:4 KJV

In all labour there is profit: but the talk of the lips *tendeth* only to penury.

Proverbs 14:23 KJV

The hand of the diligent shall bear rule: but the slothful shall be under tribute.

Proverbs 12:24 KJV

He that handleth a matter wisely shall find good: and whoso trusteth in the Lord, happy *is* he.

Proverbs 16:20 KJV

Honor those in authority over you as unto God

(2) He that walketh in his uprightness feareth the LORD: but *he that is* perverse in his ways despiseth him.

Proverbs 14:2 KJV

(22) Servants, obey in all things *your* masters according to the flesh; not with eyeservice, as menpleasers; but in singleness of heart, fearing God:

(23) And whatsoever ye do, do *it* heartily, as to the Lord, and not unto men;

Colossians 3:22-23 KJV

(5) Servants, be obedient to them that are *your* masters according to the flesh, with fear and trembling, in singleness of your heart, as unto Christ;

(6) Not with eyeservice, as menpleasers; but as the servants of Christ, doing the will of God from the heart;

(7) With good will doing service, as to the Lord, and not to men:

(8) Knowing that whatsoever good thing any man doeth, the same shall he receive of the Lord, whether *he be*

bond or free.

(9) And, ye masters, do the same things unto them, forbearing threatening: knowing that your Master also is in heaven; neither is there respect of persons with him.

(10) Finally, my brethren, be strong in the Lord, and in the power of his might.

Ephesians 6:5-10 KJV

Righteousness yields great benefits

(6) The righteousness of the upright shall deliver them: but transgressors shall be taken in *their own* naughtiness.

(17) The merciful man doeth good to his own soul: but *he that is* cruel troubleth his own flesh.

(20) They that are of a froward heart *are* abomination to the LORD: but *such as are* upright in *their* way *are* his delight.

Proverbs 11:6, 17, 20 KJV

The integrity of the upright shall guide them: but the perverseness of transgressors shall destroy them.

Proverbs 11:3 KJV

(6) Righteousness keepeth *him that is* upright in the way: but wickedness overthroweth the sinner.

(8) The ransom of a man's life *are* his riches: but the poor heareth not rebuke.

(13) Whoso despiseth the word shall be destroyed: but he that feareth the commandment shall be rewarded.

Proverbs 13:6, 8, 13 KJV

(1) Praise ye the LORD. Blessed *is* the man *that* feareth the LORD, *that* delighteth greatly in his commandments.

(2) His seed shall be mighty upon earth: the generation of the upright shall be blessed.

(5) A good man sheweth favour, and lendeth: he will

guide his affairs with discretion.

Psalm 112:1-2, 5 KJV

In the house of the righteous *is* much treasure: but in the revenues of the wicked is trouble.

Proverbs 15:6 KJV

Lying lips *are* abomination to the LORD: but they that deal truly *are* his delight.

Proverbs 12:22 KJV

And be found in him, not having mine own righteousness, which is of the law, but that which is through the faith of Christ, the righteousness which is of God by faith:

Philippians 3:9 KJV

When a man's ways please the Lord, he maketh even his enemies to be at peace with him.

Proverbs 16:7 KJV

Uniformity, self-accountability, humility and clear and fair policies are key in business

(2) Fulfil ye my joy, that ye be likeminded, having the same love, *being* of one accord, of one mind.

(3) *Let* nothing *be done* through strife or vainglory; but in lowliness of mind let esteem other better than themselves.

(12) Wherefore, my beloved, as ye have always obeyed, not as in my presence only, but now much more in my absence, work out your own salvation with fear and trembling.

(13) For it is God which worketh in you both to will and to do of *his* good pleasure.

(14) Do all things without murmurings and disputings:

(15) That ye may be blameless and harmless, the sons of God, without rebuke, in the midst of a crooked and perverse nation, among whom ye shine as lights in the world;

(21) For all seek their own, not the things which are Jesus Christ's.

Philippians 2:2-3, 12-15, 21 KJV

Pursue wisdom and stand firm on a strong foundation

(6) A scorner seeketh wisdom, and *findeth it* not: but knowledge *is* easy unto him that understandeth.

(7) Go from the presence of a foolish man, when thou perceivest not *in him* the lips of knowledge.

(8) The wisdom of the prudent *is* to understand his way: but the folly of fools *is* deceit.

(15) The simple believeth every word: but the prudent *man* looketh well to his going.

(16) A wise *man* feareth, and departeth from evil: but the fool rageth, and is confident.

(29) *He that is* slow to wrath *is* of great understanding: but *he that is* hasty of spirit exalteth folly.

Proverbs 14:6-8, 15-16, 29 KJV

Final words and closing scriptures

(6) Forsake the foolish, and live; and go in the way of understanding.

(8) Reprove not a scorner, lest he hate thee: rebuke a wise man, and he will love thee.

(9) Give *instruction* to a wise *man*, and he will be yet wiser: teach a just *man*, and he will increase in learning.

Proverbs 9:6, 8-9 KJV

Ye therefore, beloved, seeing ye know *these things* before, beware lest ye also, being led away with the error of the wicked, fall from your own stedfastness.

2 Peter 3:17 KJV

I hope all of you who are mature Christians will agree on

these things. If you disagree on some point, I believe God will make it plain to you.

Philippians 3:15 NLT

Letter from the Author

Some years ago I located the below commentary and found it quite interesting. You may have read it somewhere as well or received it in an email circulation.

Just for Fun:

Can you imagine working at the following Company? It has a little over 500 employees with the following statistics:

- 29 have been accused of spousal abuse
- 7 have been arrested for fraud
- 19 have been accused of writing bad checks
- 117 have bankrupted at least two businesses
- 3 have been arrested for assault
- 71 cannot get a credit card due to bad credit
- 14 have been arrested on drug-related charges
- 8 have been arrested for shoplifting
- 21 are current defendants in lawsuits
- In 1998 alone, 84 were stopped for drunk driving

Can you guess which organization this is?

Give up?

It's the 535 members of the United States Congress. The same group that perpetually cranks out hundreds upon hundreds of new laws designed to keep the rest of us in line.

*   *   *

I recently decided to look into it and see if I could locate the source and whether these figures were accurate. I located much back and forth commentary as to the veracity and ability to acquire these statistics. The only thing agreed upon is that the source of the information is a result of an investigation by Capitol Hill Blue, an online publication that covers federal politics.

This commentary is a reminder for me not to pattern myself after fickle legislators or the fluctuating mood of the political or social climate. I need to have a strong and reliable foundation I am able to base my business practices after. I choose The Bible as my primary guide and I strive to model my moral compass after the life of Christ.

*   *   *

To get access to tutorials, teaching videos, tips and my online courses visit my website at www.IETenantMatch.com. Become a subscriber or continue checking in so you do not miss out on any of the upcoming resources available to aid you in all your landlord endeavors. Also, for a limited time, find out how to receive a free eBook.

You may also email me at TBillBooks@yahoo.com. Please no unsolicited attachments or your entire message will be spammed.

*   *   *

(16) And moreover I saw under the sun the place of judgment, *that* wickedness *was* there; and the place of righteousness, *that* iniquity *was* there.

(17) I said in mine heart, God shall judge the righteous and the wicked: for *there is* a time there for every purpose and for every work.

Ecclesiastes 3:16-17 KJV

(16) I also noticed that under the sun there is evil in the courtroom. Yes, even the courts of law are corrupt!

(17) I said to myself, "In due season God will judge everyone, both good and bad, for all their deeds."

Ecclesiastes 3:16-17 NLT

PRAYER OF SALVATION

Landlord Droleht is the wealthiest landlord in the world. He has created his criteria and written his policies and procedures for those who want to live on his premises. He has a three step application process to live in his luxurious jurisdiction, Nevaeh. One, all applicants must recognize and believe he is the supreme ruler. Second, any potential resident must disclose and vow to renounce their past indiscretions. Lastly, they must receive Droleht as their ruler.

You do not have to live or apply for Nevaeh, there is another unfortunate alternative. This landlord has such power and authority no one and no entity can override him. It does not matter what applicants think of Droleht's rules, if they try to show up without a reservation they will be denied. Unqualified applicants have no recourse. If you would like to put your reservation in and apply for Droleht's Nevaeh, review the below terms of his Selection Criteria, you will not regret it. The accommodations are heavenly and the benefits are out of this world.

Droleht's Application Procedure & Resident Selection Criteria

For God so loved the world, that he gave his only begotten Son, that whosoever believeth in him should not perish, but have everlasting life.

John 3:16 KJV

(9) That if thou shalt confess with thy mouth the Lord Jesus, and shalt believe in thine heart that God hath raised him from the dead, thou shalt be saved.

(10) For with the heart man believeth unto righteousness; and with the mouth confession is made unto salvation.

Romans 10:9-10 KJV

(9) I am the door: by me if any man enter in, he shall be saved, and shall go in and out, and find pasture.

(10) The thief cometh not, but for to steal, and to kill, and to destroy: I am come that they might have life, and that they might have *it* more abundantly.

John 10:9-10 KJV

www.ingramcontent.com/pod-product-compliance
Lightning Source LLC
Chambersburg PA
CBHW060545200326
41521CB00007B/492